ORGANIZATIONAL DEVELOPMENT
IN THE PUBLIC SECTOR

Essentials of Public Policy and Administration Series

Series Editor Jay Shafritz
University of Pittsburgh

Westview Press proudly announces a new series of textbooks for public policy and administration courses. Written for students at both the advanced undergraduate level and graduate level, these texts follow a standard design and format which allows them to be incorporated easily into multiple courses. Each text covers a core aspect of public policy and administration that is commonly discussed in the classroom. They are written by authorities in their fields, and will serve as both core and supplemental texts.
New titles in the series include:

Organizational Development in the Public Sector
David G. Carnevale
Managing Diversity in Public Sector Workforces
Norma M. Riccucci
Comparative Public Administration and Policy
Jamil Jreisat
The Regional Governing of Metropolitan America
David Miller

ORGANIZATIONAL DEVELOPMENT IN THE PUBLIC SECTOR

David G. Carnevale

Westview

A Member of the Perseus Books Group

Essentials of Public Policy and Administration Series

Copyright © 2003 by Westview Press, A Member of the Perseus Books Group

Westview Press books are available at special discounts for bulk purchases in the United States by corporations, institutions, and other organizations. For more information, please contact the Special Markets Department at the Perseus Books Group, 11 Cambridge Center, Cambridge, MA 02142, or call (617) 252-5298, (800) 255-1514, or email j.mccrary@perseus books.com

Published in 2003 in the United States of America by Westview Press, 5500 Central Avenue, Boulder, Colorado 80301-2877, and in the United Kingdom by Westview Press, 12 Hid's Copse Road, Cumnor Hill, Oxford OX2 9JJ

Visit us on the World Wide Web at www.westviewpress.com

Library of Congress Cataloging-in-Publication Data
Carnevale, David G., 1945-
    Organizational development in the public sector / David G. Carnevale.
        p.   cm. — (Essentials of public policy and administration)
    ISBN 0-8133-4021-7 (HC : alk. paper) — ISBN 0-8133-9839-8 (Pbk. : alk. paper)
    1. Organizational change. 2. Public administration. I. Title. II. Essentials of public policy and administration series
JF1525.O73 C37 2002
352.3'67—dc21   2002005072

The paper used in this publication meets the requirements of the American National Standard for Permanence of Paper for Printed Library Materials Z39.48-1984.

10   9   8   7   6   5   4   3   2   1—05   04   03   02

For Isabella, Emma, Amanda, and Simon

CONTENTS

LIST OF FIGURES

PREFACE AND ACKNOWLEDGMENTS

Purpose and Origins

This text can be used as a stand-alone treatment of Organizational Development (OD). The book is also an excellent supplement to traditional textbooks in the field and is a good addition to readings in organizational behavior and principles of management. This book provides the essentials of OD. It also provides more; the strength of the book is its strong handling of the field's underlying values and assumptions.

As a field of study, OD seems enamored of technical interventions in organizations. I believe there is a limit to the number of procedures that people can grasp. I also think the truth of practice is that intervention methods overlap and collapse into hybrid approaches dictated by the realities of the situation. Readers of books about OD can miss appreciating the complicated nature of practice. Techniques are tools. Success in practice means keeping intervention methods in perspective while remaining faithful to core concepts of the field. Students may fail to see the core values that inform practice. People can be captured in what some public administrationists characterize as realizing the "triumph of techniques over purpose." To counter the forces of technicism, the spiritual essence of OD requires ongoing notice. This book takes the position that once people have a good sense of what OD is fundamentally about, the "moves" or methods naturally follow.

What matters in the end are the underlying attitudes, values, and assumptions that lie at the heart of OD. A superficial methods orientation leaves the OD practitioner armed only with what has cynically been characterized as the usual "OD bag of tricks." All practitioners use a toolkit, but it is the ongoing diagnosis of the essence of the situation that informs the content and process of practice. This text appreciates OD as a craft, artistry in action.

When I teach mediation or negotiation to students, for example, they want to know the "moves." They are often disappointed when I tell them that there are thousands of situations, points of attack, and just as many moves. No one can master or memorize what to do in every situation. The best thing is to understand the process itself, to get a feel for what is valued, to know assumptions, and, most of all, be fully in touch with one's own attitude. When that happens, no matter the situation, the values and sense of mission will get them through. Fundamental psychological self-awareness drives attitude that influences behavior. OD practitioners do not get all tied up thinking about what to do. They have a feel for the physics of the moment and react reflectively and effectively in-action.

Readers need to appreciate that OD has a point of view about the human side of enterprise (to borrow an apt phrase). OD is a philosophy about the development of people. There are a number of venues where human growth might occur. OD focuses on the workplace and recognizes the value of work as developmental, not just of persons' skills and abilities, but also the realization of their authentic selves. It is in doing work that people may discover themselves, if they have some measure of freedom.

Some would assert it is all a matter of balance, taking care of the instrumental needs of organizations and the requirements of the human element. Balance is typically called for when two ideas—in this case task and relationship—appear at odds. This book rejects balance. It shades to the human side; recognizing that organizations are indeed social systems and nothing good gets done without the support and cooperation of people. In other words, this book takes a stance for the human relations perspective of organizations. I ask What is an economy for? How should organizations behave in a democratic society? What is the positive potential of working experience in human development? Getting good work done is essential and I do not mean to dismiss its import, but OD has a fundamental spirit that extols the importance of the human factor in getting exceptional work accomplished and it is the standpoint taken here.

The book covers many of the usual OD topics such as Action Research, group dynamics, and coverage of OD as a field of study. It incorporates some things that make it distinctive. There is considerable treatment of change, resistance to change, and defensive conduct concerning transformation in organizations. This is a major issue in practice and I wanted to give it substantial attention here. The book also pays a good deal of attention to conflict resolution, a topic that has become increasingly important in organizational development. Change begets conflict and it is an issue that warrants good attention. Issues such as leadership, trust, systems theory, public-private differences, process consultation, the emergence of OD as a counterpoint to classic bureaucratic management methods, a brief history of modern management reform and the idea of empowerment, positive and negative aspects of group dynamics, trust, hierarchy, labor relations, and other issues are addressed.

Audience

People interested in Organizational Development will obviously be interested in the book as a stand-alone treatment of the field or as a supplemental text to other books used in OD, organizational behavior, or organizational theory. The text is highly readable and covers a range of topics in a field that is sometimes difficult to describe. Recently I agreed to work with a city on their problems with three unions and their nonunion employees in general. We were trying to figure out how I might explain my entrance into the problem. If we keyed in on labor relations directly, it was risky. I said that we could call the approach "Organizational Development." The city manager was delighted and said, "That's great, nobody knows what that really means!" After reading this book, it is my hope that people will know what it means, not just in theory but also in practice. What OD is fundamentally about is made clear and that ultimately is its primary value.

Overview

Chapter 1 defines Organizational Development (OD) and discusses the philosophy of OD in terms of its assumptions and values. The idea that OD represents something of a paradigm shift away from the bureaucratic ideal of organization structures and its close cousin scientific management are discussed at some length. Major OD pioneers are profiled and the importance of systems theory is outlined. Some criticisms of OD are presented and addressed. The modern age of management reform is described and compared to the tenets of OD.

Chapter 2 addresses organizational development and the field of public administration. The basic questions are whether OD practice is the same in public and private jurisdictions, what differences might exist depending on sector, and whether those distinctions are meaningful. Stories from the author's consulting experience are used to demonstrate how public OD does differ from private undertakings. Moreover, the operating context of the public OD practitioner is found to be distinctive in ways related to the operating domain of the typical public enterprise. The argument is that public OD is more difficult to practice than its private counterpart, and, despite that view, there is some evidence that public OD may be more successful.

Chapter 3 addresses the issue of change in organizations. The psychology of resistance to change receives lengthy treatment. Why "unfreezing" persons from their mind-sets is easier in theory than practice receives good attention. How to overcome defensive conduct is outlined as well as leading change. The role of process consultation (PC) is detailed as a good way to overcome resistance to change and to build trust.

Chapter 4 relates change, growth, and learning. OD has been invested in the idea of human capital development for some time. In a sense, that is a superficial, instrumental concern. Self-awareness is a form of learning too and is part of a deeper process. Cutting-edge organizations support human capital and personal development of employees. However, learning organizations only exist because of power. Knowledge is power, as the saying goes, but only if power permits it to be. Power decides knowledge and not the other way around. That is an important point discussed in this chapter. The whole issue of the seeds of employee disempowerment and the restoration of respect for employee know-how is examined.

Chapter 5 deals with groups and group processes since they are the forerunners of teams in organizations. The upside or positive effects of groups are examined and so are the downside tendencies. Groups are not always functional and excessive cohesion in a group or team may be dysfunctional. A brief revisit is made to the history of management philosophy at the turn of the century to contrast the ideas of management revival that began enthusiastically in the 1980s. The context of this discussion is the ongoing debate in public administration about the new public management. Group process and decision models are then elaborated.

Chapter 6 concerns conflict resolution. Social systems are full of conflict and it is common that the OD change agent faces the situation of a need for team building or helping to repair interpersonal, intra-unit, and interunit difficulties. The escalation tendencies of conflict are outlined. The core of the chapter concerns "dialogue" or the type of communication necessary to help people resolve differences. A model of dialogue is submitted and explained.

Chapter 7 summarizes the basic theoretical ideas in the book and addresses several topics, however briefly, that any OD text must speak to such as hierarchy, leadership, trust, labor relations, power, and politics, and makes conclusions about OD, its past, and future prospects.

Acknowledgments

I would like to thank a number of people who helped influence my feelings about organizational development and writing a book about it. First, my students over the past three years in the Human Relations Department at the University of Oklahoma have had a great influence with respect to my thinking about this topic. I teach the OD course twice a year. As every professor knows, teaching a course forces one to get the story right, to make sense of the material, to see what works and what does not, and to get feedback from people. Students have shown me that OD represents the natural values and aspirations of people at work. They have validated the subject for me. I want to thank my friend Ralph Hummel who never lets go of his faith in front-line workers and what they know. I want to thank all the organizations that have invited me to train or work with staff in some way to help solve some sort of problem. I have learned much in practice. My experiences reaffirm my belief that employees know the problems and the answers. I am constantly amazed that staff ideas on flip charts contain the same themes. What people understand is an organizational resource if it is liberated. I want to thank Susan Medina for doing the bibliographic work for the book and I want to especially thank Terry Goodson, my ally and former student, who could not do enough for me in terms of taking notes in all of my classes and getting the graphics together on disk. I owe Charles Bender much for coming to my aid on short notice and helping me get this work to press. I want to thank my colleagues in the Human Relations Department for helping me, as a public administrator, to learn more about the psychology of people and to appreciate the diversity of knowledge, mind-sets, and values spinning about in social systems. Finally, I want to say a word to my OD professor at Florida State, Frank Sherwood. Professor Sherwood had to contend with my stubbornness in not accepting OD as a valid topic for study because, as a trade unionist, I thought it was manipulative and left workers essentially powerless. I have learned much since my student days twelve years ago. I have changed not only how I feel about OD but how I teach and practice negotiation and mediation. Professor Sherwood should regard me as a late bloomer.

David G. Carnevale
Norman, Oklahoma

ACRONYMS

ADR	Alternative Dispute Resolution
AFSCME	American Federation of State, County, and Municipal Employees
AR	Action Research
IBB	Interest-Based Bargaining
LGIMs	Large Group Interaction Methods
NGT	Nominal Group Technique
NPM	New Public Management
NTDS	National Training and Development Service
NTL	National Training Laboratories
OD	Organizational Development
PAR	*Public Administrative Review*
PC	Process Consultation
QWL	Quality of Work Life
STS	Sociotechnical systems
TL	Transformational Leadership
TQM	Total Quality Management

1

Organizational Development: Assumptions and Values

Organizational Development (OD) can be defined in several ways but all explanations contain common elements. OD is seen as an effort to deal with or initiate change in organizational cultures through a technology known as *Action Research* (AR). Action Research is a method of collaboration between a change agent and members of an organizational system. The central objective of AR is to expedite the diagnosis of organization problems and to encourage strategies that equip organizational members to learn how to cope with their own difficulties. OD is underscored by a belief that organizational members own their own problems and are responsible for finding solutions to them. OD does not "fix" people through the use of outside consultants. Actions selected by organizational members are planned and underpinned by established norms of behavioral science and a set of optimistic values and assumptions about human capacities. Organizational Development pays particular attention to organizational processes or the way things are done, not just what is done. OD essentially deals with a false paradox, that the development of people in organizations is a separate and incompatible concern from the productive issues of the organization itself (French and Bell, 1999; Bennis, 1969; Golembiewski, 1985; Bruce and Wyman, 1998).

Organizational Development is a philosophy. It is a certain way of thinking about people at work. It represents a set of values and assumptions. At bottom, OD epitomizes democratic values. It gives employees the opportunity to participate in organizational decision-making and reduces reliance on hierarchical power as the sole arbiter of the correctness of decisions. It gives staff effective voice. What employees believe and express becomes crucial data to recast work systems. OD manifests a normative-reeducative educational philosophy because it encourages individuals and groups to reexamine core values, beliefs, and operating assumptions about themselves, other people, and the way that their organizations function. Normative reeducation opens the door to learning.

OD shifts away from the idea that elites ensconced at the top of bureaucratic pyramids possess superior knowledge for all situations. OD prizes all types of know-how. Experiential wisdom, for example, is considered valuable and is the intuition that often arises from it. OD is not solely attached to rational methods of problem solving and the tenets of idealism. It embraces the experience of realism as well.

Ultimately, OD is a social technology that helps human systems remain competitive in an era where organizational operating domains are turbulent and all labor systems are wide open to the forces of change. Development means change and it requires learning.

Bennis (1969, p. 15) describes the normative values of OD change agents as:

- Improvement in interpersonal competence.
- A shift in values so that human factors and feelings come to be considered legitimate.
- Development of increased understanding between and within working groups in order to reduce tensions.
- Development of more effective team "management," that is, the capacity . . . for functional groups to work more competently.
- Development of better methods of conflict "resolution." Rather than the usual bureaucratic methods that rely mainly on suppression, compromise, and unprincipled power, more rational and open methods of conflict resolution are sought.
- Development of organic rather than mechanical systems. This is a strong reaction against the idea of organizations as mechanisms which managers work "on," like pushing buttons . . .

Tannenbaum and Davis (1969, pp. 67–83) suggest that OD represents a paradigm shift away from traditional bureaucratic, mechanistic institutions that prize instrumental values at the expense of a more developmental and sanguine view of people. They suggest movement:

- Away from a view of people as essentially bad toward a view of people as basically good.
- Away from avoidance of negative evaluation of individuals toward confirming them as human beings.
- Away from a view of individuals as fixed, toward seeing them as being in process.
- Away from resisting and fearing individual differences toward accepting and utilizing them.
- Away from utilizing an individual primarily with reference to his or her job description toward viewing an individual as a whole person.
- Away from walling off the expression of feelings toward making possible both appropriate expression and effective use.
- Away from maskmanship and game playing toward authentic behavior.
- Away from the use of status for maintaining power and personal prestige toward use of status for organizationally relevant purposes.
- Away from distrusting people toward trusting them.
- Away from avoiding facing others with relevant data toward making appropriate confrontation.
- Away from avoidance of risk taking toward willingness to risk.
- Away from a view of process work as being unproductive effort toward seeing it as essential to effective task accomplishment.
- Away from a primary emphasis on competition toward a much greater emphasis on collaboration.

Organizational Development may be based on the touchstone of behavioral science, but it embraces a healthy intuitive, spiritual, and felt sense of judgment to find the right thing to do.

A General History of Management Thinking and OD[1]

Organizational Development has deep roots. The emergence of Organizational Development closely parallels the evolution of management thinking during the twentieth century. OD is an antidote to the widespread management consensus that command and control from the upper reaches of hierarchies is the best path to organizational effectiveness. At bottom, OD's coming forth is intimately connected to questions about the value of different kinds of knowledge at work. Every organizational theory is also a theory of knowledge and vice versa (Thayer, 1980, p. 113).

Frederick Taylor[2]

At the beginning of the twentieth century, organizations competed on the basis of mass production that involved manufacturing high volumes of standardized goods and services at the lowest possible price. Mass production systems were responsive to the requirements of America's early industrialization period. In the public sector, a similar objective was to ensure that all Americans had access to mass-produced services such as education, health care, and law enforcement. Mass production methods were successful in providing Americans with a standard of living and quality of life unmatched in most parts of the world.

The unparalleled success of mass production methods in turn-of-the-century America is appropriately credited to the contribution of Frederick Taylor's (1911) scientific management, the classic set of ideas used to rationalize work. Scientific management is fueled by the rational bias that work can be reduced to an engineered blueprint and totally controlled based on scientific knowledge. Taylorist methods support the basic aims of mass production by bringing all aspects of work under strict control. It is a parsimonious model of organizational management driven by efficiency and economy values. There is no wasted motion, no variation from the standard way of doing things, and complete obedience to the knowledge imperatives that arise from outside doing the actual work.

Public management admired scientific management and fully embraced business values of efficiency, economy, and top-down control. The goal of public administration was to model itself after the way business conducted its affairs (Wilson, 1887). The upshot of this mindset established once and for all that business management was in every way superior to public administration. The cry to make government more businesslike echoes even today.

Scientific management caused employees to lose command over the full expression of their work. The philosophy of science was enlisted to separate work into two parts—conception and execution. Through the use of analytic techniques like time-and-motion studies, the mental aspects of work were separated from their physical manifestations. Where once staff enjoyed a broad "scope of action" over their jobs, they were now deskilled, reduced to carrying out the directives of engineers.[3] The consequences proved to be severe for frontline workers. As Braverman (1974, p. 125) notes, "hand and brain become not just separated, but divided and hostile, and the human unity of hand and brain turns into its opposite, something less than human." Workers became cogs in the machine, alienated from their work, their coworkers, and, ultimately, from themselves. The machine is not necessarily a factory. It can be a government organization.

Weberian Ideal-Type Bureaucracy

In 1922, the German sociologist Max Weber described "bureaucracy" as the perfect way to structure and manage organizations. The ideal-type bureaucracy is hierarchical, features a rigorous chain of command, specialization of tasks, division of labor, procedures and rules to accomplish the work, selection and promotion of employees based on performance, impartial treatment of customers and clients, and a general impersonality with regard to human relations. It is mechanistic.

It was in this machinelike organization that the principles of scientific philosophy were thrust. The combination of scientific management and ideal-type bureaucracy were perfectly suited and served as a robust platform to launch America into the twentieth century as an industrial power. There were salutary effects. Jobs were provided for immigrants and the quality of life was uplifted for many Americans. Projects on a grand scale were accomplished. The rationalized bureaucratic organization spurred America's takeoff period as a modern economy and superpower.

There were, however, unintended consequences on the job. So much attention was paid to the accomplishment of instrumental objectives in organizations that human expectations about work were largely ignored. Specifically, the meaning of work was eroded. Alienation and unrest among workers began to rise as a result of the dominance of the bureaucratic mechanism. There was a marked rise in "labor troubles." It was agreed that something had to be done. The machine was losing productive capacity. Enter industrial psychology, Human Relations, and OD (Taylor, 1911; Weber, Gerth, and Mills, 1946; French and Bell, 1999).

Responding to Taylor's call for a "mental revolution," Chris Argyris, a prominent spokesperson for the values of OD, wrote:

> ... these experts have provided little insight into why they believe that people should undergo a "mental revolution"; or why esprit de corps is necessary if the principles are to succeed. The only hints found are that resistance to scientific management occurs because human beings are what they are, or "because it's human nature." But, why does "human nature" resist formal organizational principles? Perhaps there is something inherent in the principles which cause human resistance. (1957, p. 57)

Argyris captures the problem perfectly. Are productive and employee concerns compatible? Can effectiveness mean accomplishment of instrumental concerns and promote staff growth and development at the same time? Is the choice between being "hard" or "soft" or is there another way to get things done that serves both productive and human needs?

The Human Relations Counterpoint

From 1927 to 1932 the Hawthorne Studies were conducted at the Hawthorne plant of the Western Electric Company. The investigation was initiated to discover the effects of physical factors on work performance but researchers came away understanding there was much more going on with the workforce that was not fully appreciated in classic organization theory. It shifted focus away from controlling hierarchies to the social-psychological needs of employees. It is seen as the seminal event that started what is characterized as the Human Relations school of organizational theory. From the classicists' point of view, the Hawthorne experiments were initially seen as failures. To the sharper eyes of the interpretivists, the tests were a success because they revealed that how employees interpreted events made a difference in how they worked. There was symbolic meaning in how organizations were operated that could not be ignored.

Human Relations drew management's attention to the phenomenological aspects of organizational life. The meaning of work to people slowly moved onto the stage. Organizations were inspired to treat workers like adults, not children (Argyris, 1957). They were encouraged to satisfy their needs (Maslow, 1965; Herzberg, 1966). They were energized to involve them in decisions about how the work was done (Likert, 1961), to better integrate technological and social systems in the workplace (Trist and Bamforth, 1951), and to provide employees with more interesting, challenging, and meaningful work (Hackman and Oldham, 1980). Perhaps the best description of the contrast between traditional management methods and the kind suggested by human relationists is found in Douglas McGregor's *The Human Side of Enterprise* (1960). It contrasted management assumptions associated with classic management theory—Theory X—with a style more consistent with Human Relations and OD values—Theory Y. The former theory repressed human potential on the job whereas the latter trusted employees to take on responsibility if given the chance. Further, Chester Barnard (1938) established the idea that organizations were social systems and the manager's job was to gain people's cooperation. Overall, there is a basic theme: people matter.

All of the theorists I have mentioned owe much to the Hawthorne researchers, especially Elton Mayo, who was hostile to the idea that technical and material advancement alone composed the definition of progress. He was not preoccupied with problems of managerial authority and mechanized production. He was a reactionary who believed that techniques had led to social dislocation, lack of cooperation, and other forms of unrest. He was deeply concerned about the human and social problems created by the new industrial civilization.

Looking back over the early Human Relations/OD literature, one sees certain themes: A package of optimistic assumptions about the potential of people; the faith that people know something about the work and that their know-how has value to the organization; an antibureaucratic bent; and a drive to treat staff as responsible adults who can make real contributions at work. People are viewed as motivated by needs for self-development, interesting and meaningful work, a role in goal setting, and good relations with coworkers. It is believed that leaders are likely to achieve more by less autocratic rule-driven styles in favor of more flexible and democratic approaches. The literature acknowledges the significance of group processes and teamwork. The human processes of organizations are seen as powerful. Eventually, learning in organizations will find its place as an extension of these ideas. The concept that there is a spiritual aspect to organizational life will also find a niche. Taken together, these values are diametrically different from the assumptions of the classic scientific bureaucratic ideal that dominated the organizational landscape at the beginning of the twentieth century.[4]

Deepening the OD Connection

Principal among the catalysts for the advancement of OD was Kurt Lewin, an experimental social psychologist who thought in systems terms, force fields, and the fundamental stages of change.

Lewin's contributions to the field of Organizational Development are considerable. Four of his ideas in particular are significant. First, Lewin recognized organizations as systems of contradictory forces that produce the status quo. It is a paradoxical view. Using a technique known as "force field analysis," Lewin (1947) demonstrated how, in any domain, dynamics are at work pushing and pulling against one another. To change a situation, the equilibrium point between the forces has to be adjusted. The value of the idea is that force field analysis gives organizations a way to identify the factors that constitute the positive and negative physics of their situations and a way to change them. Force field analysis continues to be used today as a viable facilitation mechanism to uncover the levers for change. Once the contending energies are revealed, actions increasing positive pressures or reducing negative or blocking factors can be undertaken.

Lewin's second contribution is the description of change as a rough three-step process, *unfreezing, moving (changing),* and *refreezing.* It is a simple concept but captures the essentials of the change succession. Unfreezing involves disconfirming people of their rigid ideas, misperceptions, and delusions about the nature of reality. It is a painful sequence and naturally engenders resistance. People are fearful of change. It helps if they have some part in establishing its conditions. It is also comforting if employees are provided a measure of psychological safety during the change process.

During the unfreezing stage, individuals undergo a cognitive restructuring of established mind-sets and replace them with fresh hypotheses about the possibility and prospects of change. Rethinking one's values and beliefs is difficult to actualize. As Quinn notes, "When we see the need for deep change, we usually see it as something that needs to take place in someone else" (1996, p. 11). One of the realities of organizational culture, for instance, is that it operates much like the psychological unconscious that automatically protects the status quo. Stepping into the unknown has its risks and change agents know too well how difficult it is to break through resistance to change and inculcate new operative norms in individuals, groups, and organizations. Normative reeducation of persons fearful of what change may bring to their lives is a daunting enterprise in practice. The third step in the change process is "refreezing," wherein new values, beliefs, and behaviors are stabilized. Both stability and renewal are simultaneously established.

Lewin's three-step change process implies a certain static quality. That is misleading. Individuals, groups, and organizations constantly face this trial. Life is difficult and turbulent; there is no time when matters are settled once and for all. Change is an ongoing, vigorous process; it is the nature of things. Individuals who face the truth of their situations have a better chance of coping and surviving than those who do not make the effort to fit their behaviors with reality.

Supporting people in confronting the need for personal and organizational transformation is one of the principal goals of the OD change agent. The idea is to help people learn to cope with the realities of their situations, not to hold out the false hope of controlling their existences.

Lewin's work comes together in the idea of Action Research (AR), which can be characterized as the core technology of Organizational Development. It embodies all the values of OD and is the basis of most "interventions" used by change agents. French (1969, p. 26) describes Action Research in the following way:

> The key aspects of the model are diagnosis, data gathering, and feedback to the client group, data discussion and work by the client group, action planning, and action. The sequence tends to cyclical, with the focus on new or advanced problems as the client group learns to work more effectively together.

The process is iterative. The group keeps action planning, taking action, processing feedback, and making adjustments in strategy as necessary. It is important to note that the data being analyzed can come from the group itself. For example, in a team-building session a group might be asked What is it that we do well? What do we need to improve? If there were one thing we could do to improve the situation, what might it be? These questions generate sufficient data to initiate the remaining steps of the AR cycle. In sum, Action Research embodies the fundamental values of OD. It is democratic in that it allows effective employee voice and is inclusive. It is optimistic that people can learn to solve their own problems. It is humanistic in that it encourages the development of people and the realization of their potential. Its genesis owes much to Kurt Lewin.

Lewin's fourth contribution stems from his collaboration with Ronald Lippitt, Leland Bradford, and Kenneth Benne at the Commission on Community Interrelations of the American Jewish Congress, which gave rise to "T-Groups" during the post–World War II years. During a training endeavor the staff would meet to discuss what had transpired each day. Participants found out about the meetings and asked to attend. The researchers were initially anxious about sharing data about people with them in the room, but overcame their trepredations and let people come in and talk about the interpretations of data about them. The exchanges were powerful and helpful to all of the participants. What transpired was an awareness that learning could occur among all participants, as well as group building, these days known as team building; all the actors had an effective voice in interpreting the motivation and meaning of the day's behaviors. The idea of open group meetings shifted OD from skill training to an emphasis on interpersonal learning. This in turn led to the development of the National Training Laboratories (NTL) and the so-called "laboratory method," also known as "human relations training," "group dynamics," and "executive development" programs (McGill, 1974; Burke, 1982).

Through T-Groups and the work of the National Training Laboratories, OD had turned a corner that emphasized different processes and experiences. Training was less about imparting information than people taking responsibility for learning through interactions with other persons, receiving feedback, and processing data about themselves. This is an entirely different type of learning model and, at bottom, is Action Research realized.

Systems Theory

Another evolutionary advance in Organizational Development is the influence of systems theory. Systems theory envisions organizations and their employees open to and influenced by their environments. It is posited that organizations gather input from their environments and transform them into output. The organization measures output against established goals and objectives. The data on accomplishments establish feedback loops or learning about what can be done to improve organizational performance. Organizational leaders can pursue greater input (we need more resources) or transform manipulation of throughput processes (we need to manage things differently). The cycle repeats itself. Much of systems theory is reminiscent of Lewin, that is, forces swarm about organizations that require adjustment depending on their nature.

Environmental forces that affect input and output are the perceived value of the organization's mission or product demand. External political, legal, social, economic, technological, and social forces also play their part. Internally, the relevant physics relate to how work processes are established, the quality of the reward and incentive system, leadership style, work schedules, the extent of organizational learning processes, employee skills, and so on. The principal idea is that organizations and the people in them exist in an organic world and they have to change and adapt to contingencies in their operating domains. Both are either open or closed to their environments (Bertalanffy, 1950, 1956).

"Open systems thinking" has had significant import for OD because it encourages learning and shared vision in terms of the whole rather than just parts (Senge, 1990). It transcends endless complexity and cautions that what happens in one part of a system can have consequences elsewhere. It means that just working on one part of the culture or relying on one type of intervention in the hope that it will reverberate positively throughout a large interdependent system cannot transform organizations. To change a system means to change the entire system, not just a part of it (French and Bell, 1999).

There is a major implication for OD in the systems perspective that organizational leaders and their change agents sometimes fail to appreciate. Contingencies in external and internal systems are customarily beyond the control of change advocates, no matter how well motivated. For example, conducting a survey, a single team-building retreat, installing a new incentive and reward system, and facilitating a workshop on conflict resolution over the course of a year will not usually yield a large system change or deep alterations in an organization's culture. In short, human work systems are complex and changing them involves persistent intervening over long periods of time to achieve results. In systems theory, there is no quick fix (Kilmann, 1984).

Persisting Beyond Negative Labels

To a real extent, all these ideas about shifting the paradigm of how to construct and manage organizations did have some effect. Still, Human Relations and its OD prodigy were sometimes seen as "soft" techniques to make people feel better about their jobs rather than giving them genuine voice in what should be done and how. Human Relations and its OD subcomponent were often criticized as manipulative management methods that scrupulously avoided questions of power. They were perceived as cynical devices to help management avoid labor troubles. They were accused of providing a veneer of harmony to mask the real conflict rampant in organizations. The criticism has some merit. There is no doubt that many organizations were committed to a type of "pseudo-participation" aimed at increasing morale without changing the fundamental power relations that ruled the workplace. It was this apparent sham about power that fueled the criticisms of radical humanists and antiorganizational theorists who detested programs like OD (some known under the rubric of Quality of Working Life) as servants of functionalism—obstructions to real change (Burrell and Morgan, 1979).

OD values represented something more than its critics could wave away, despite the fact that some organizational leaders saw OD as a way to manipulate staff into feeling good and working harder without benefiting in any meaningfully developmental way. OD's fundamental values and its champions for changing organizations to make them better persisted. The unalterable truth is that OD change agents shared the idea that there needed to be an employee-centered counterforce to the authoritarian bent of traditional command and control approaches to management. They were humanists and existentialists, passionate about human development. They were optimistic because they believed that people will take responsibility for their own problems and have the wherewithal to do something about their conditions. Nonetheless, the debate about OD being "soft" versus "hard" persists and reveals much about the assumptions about people found in the psychology of persons on both sides of the debate. Every management reform (perhaps with the exception of reengineering organizations) carries OD values as part of their repertoire of productivity-enhancing initiatives. The evidence is overwhelming. The way people are treated has hard consequences for the bottom line.

Even though OD theorists and practitioners demonstrated in case after case that there was no automatic disconnect between treating staff with respect and realizing productive organizational outcomes, OD was labeled as "touchy-feely." A colleague of mine, an unbending positivist, once characterized OD as the "Dale Carnegie Paradigm" or "Dare to Be Great" archetype. This masked his constant complaining that there were numerous problems in the department that could be fixed if we were just given some say. There was a kind of masculine mind-set that real organizations were commanded and controlled, and that tough decisionmaking was the mark of the top-notch, usually male, executive. "Tough but fair" was the order of the day. It is authoritarian. Still, OD persisted. Case after case demonstrated that productivity can be high, people can develop, cultures can be healthy, and work can have positive meaning for those who do it.

Competitiveness Pushes the Door Wide Open for OD Values

Events in the 1980s were to starkly demonstrate that how employees are involved in organizational processes is the signal factor in organizational success. Once and for all, the idea that concentration on instrumental tasks alone is the key to success was thoroughly discredited.

To change organizations, there needs to be a fresh focus on knowledge and the locus of power. The novel idea is that there are all types of knowledge in organizations, not just the one embraced by the dominant hierarchical coalition. Different ways of appreciating reality is grounded in different experiences, essences, and types of existence. There are lots of realities in every organization because there are lots of different people performing different roles. Each individual has a distinct experience outside of any job description or organizational rule. This is what Taylor missed. The trick for high performance is to honor these different experiences—ways of knowing, know-how, and learning—and translate among them to be able to judge the best course in a problematic situation based on reality, not rule from above—one kind of knowing. Power can decide knowledge but that obliterates the wisdom of the statement that knowledge is power. Organizations that do not recognize this cannot learn and they are incapable of change.

The New Era of Reform

In the early 1980s, American industry went through a difficult economic downturn. Unlike previous recessions, this one signaled serious problems with the way American organizations were led and managed. The nation was surprised and battered by the alarming drop in America's competitiveness. Quantity production, once the holy grail of public and private management, was replaced by a new set of competitive standards. These included variety, customization, convenience, timeliness, and especially quality (Carnevale, 1990). These new competitive principles demanded a different management philosophy, one based on quality knowledge.

The problems facing business paralleled those facing government at precisely the same time. Taxpayer revolts in Massachusetts and California and the election of Ronald Reagan signaled dramatic changes in the operations of government. It too was expected to change how to deal with "customers."[5]

Because of the decline in American competitiveness, American management in government and business enthusiastically embraced an eclectic set of ideas to improve organizational performance. Some of the most salient ideas deal with excellence (Peters and Waterman, 1982), Japanese management techniques (Ouchi, 1981), Total Quality Management (TQM) programs (Deming, 1986; Juran, 1988), changing organizational culture (Deal and Kennedy, 1982), improving organizational learning (Senge, 1990), and government-oriented strategies (Osborne and Gaebler, 1992; Gore, 1993).

The new approach involved several core concepts.

1. *Customer or client satisfaction is the primary goal of the organization.* The issue of what an appropriate definition of "customer" means in government continues to be problematic although most explanations would embrace the idea of taxpayers as customers whether or not they are the direct beneficiaries of the goods and services produced by government.

2. *There is a strong commitment to human capital development.* The idea that, in open systems, organizations must learn and they cannot if internal groups and individuals are unable to do so (Senge, 1990).

3. *Continuous improvement customarily borne of the ideas of various forms of work teams is a paramount system goal.* Systems and processes are the objects of improvement, not correcting or

punishing the behavior of individuals or creating blaming-type work climates.

4. *There is an enthusiastic pledge to employee involvement and partic-ipation in all kinds of forms.* Staff is given the chance to generate ideas, identify priorities, and take action to solve problems. There is less "telling" and more questioning about what should be done in a particular circumstance.

5. *Common vision is prized.* The creation of shared vision is the bedrock of the two leadership styles with the most currency these days—transformational (Bass, 1985) and charismatic (Conger, 1989) leadership methods.

6. *Government organizations are encouraged to be entrepreneurial* (Os-borne and Gaebler, 1992). This means that government must aggressively come up with ways to raise capital, improve ser-vices, compete with private vendors, and think in terms of be-ing active participants in markets. Governments make things happen. They cannot survive as passive institutions.

7. *Organizational culture becomes the rage.* According to Kilmann and associates, "Culture is to the organization what personal-ity is to individual—a hidden, yet unifying theme that pro-vides meaning, direction, and mobilization" (1985, p. ix). Studies of culture inevitably lead to issues of change in organi-zations, the fundamental business of OD. It also looks to the underlying psychology of people and their reactions to the practices of organizations as crucial in their loyalty, identifica-tion, and commitment to the organization and its mission.

8. *Empowerment.* Of all the phrases that hold the new paradigm together, none is so common as the commitment to "empow-erment" or the notion that those closest to the customer and client should have effective voice and discretion in dealing with organizational problems down the line. Empowerment occurs in individuals and typically in teams. It is sold as revo-lutionary. It certainly has implications for shifting the center of gravity of the power of knowledge in organizations. But what must be remembered is that to em-power means that sometime before staff were dis-empowered.

All of these ideas owe their pedigree in one way or another to earlier Human Relations and OD assumptions about people and work. Guillén observes:

> These authors conceive of organizational cultures as "systems of informal rules," and a "strong culture" is thought to enable people to feel better about what they do, so they are more likely to work harder. The business firm is seen as community, almost to the exclusion of all other possible group memberships that workers may have. The buzzwords of the organization culture paradigm include *sense of belonging, integrative leadership, organizational climate, involvement, participation, loyalty, commitment, harmony, interdependence, cohesiveness,* and *team spirit.* Human relations techniques such as interviews, social observation, group dynamics, and morale surveys are proposed to diagnose the problem and foster an atmosphere of cooperation in the workplace. The echoes of the Human Relations paradigm could not resonate louder. (1995, pp. 289–290)

Conclusion

Organizational Development is a values-loaded technology (Golembiewski, 1985). It is meant to improve the performance of organizations. It is not solely concerned with the instrumental objectives of organizations. OD holds that the expressive needs of people at work have their place too. That does not mean that OD is "soft" with little regard for productive issues. It is built on evidence that task and relationship behaviors are the crucial pieces in the recipe for high-performing work organizations. It embraces individuals and the organization as intimately related and necessary to the other. It transcends bipolar or dualistic thinking that paying attention to just half the task and relationship equation is sufficient to achieve high performance.

The OD perspective shadows the development of management thinking since the beginning of the last century. It is counterpower to the autocratic, top-down bureaucratic machine that stripped employees of meaningful control of their work. It intends to humanize workplaces, recognizing that people have a right to some measure of self-development at work. It encourages democracy on the shop floor and in the office. Finally, it is optimistic that people can do good work given a chance.

OD values are still grudgingly embraced. Although they make sense to people, they are not normally experienced. They seem like pleasant abstractions. The typical workplace is fraught with conflict, back-biting, destructive ambition, and leaders whose espoused theories and theories of action are incongruent. Trust is lower than it might be and people feel more and more insecure in the new economy, where the psychological contract guarantees very little in the long term even though material gain is everywhere. Meaning is lost. The problem is how to get the intellectual abstractions of Human Relations into practice through OD.

In the next chapter, I examine Organizational Development in the public sector. Is the problem of changing public organizations the same as altering the business enterprise? Can OD be successful in government? What are the strengths and limitations of context?

Notes

1. I am heavily indebted for the knowledge argument to Ralph Hummel. We have talked endlessly about this idea and have collaborated on several conference papers and a book draft concerning how the driving force underlying management reforms in the past century has been based on an attempt to embrace experiential know-how without conceding hierarchical power. We see management reforms as a struggle between idealism supported by science and realism. As the ensuing discussion will demonstrate, OD is about legitimizing staff knowledge down the line and empowering people in more than superficial ways. It endorses experiential know-how and the tenets of realism. The discussion of the historical development of OD will reflect the tie between issues of knowledge and power. The values of OD serve a particular purpose. They aim to get people involved at work because they know something. They have something to contribute and it is valuable for productive purposes. If knowledge is indeed power, it is the power to actualize and to contribute. It is about the liberation of employee know-how.

2. The case of Frederick Taylor is interesting. Much of the literature casts him as a villain who did much damage to workers and was insensitive to their needs. That view is somewhat unfair. His intentions were admirable. He wanted to bring a rational scheme to the chaos of the industrial plant in a way that would prevent management from treating staff in an entirely arbitrary

fashion. He died a bitter man, feeling misunderstood. It is arguable that his intentions were more noble than not, but his methods were hijacked by management for their own designs (compare with Weisbord, 1987; Schachter, 1989).

3. It is astounding how much of the classical school of management thinking owes its pedigree to the work of assorted engineers. The engineering mentality leaves little room for humanism in social systems.

4. "Human Relations" is used as an umbrella concept at this point in the text to capture the intended shift away from strict rationalism of work toward concern with the meaning of labor to staff and their involvement in both its conception and execution. Many, if not all, of the human relation writers identified so far are members of the Organizational Development school—some more self-consciously than others. This introductory chapter sets the history of the development of management thinking and reform in the twentieth century. Human Relations will continue to be used to house authors who also fit the OD paradigm. After the general historical overview is established, the next chapter will pay attention to OD in the public sector.

5. The following discussion focuses mainly on the historical development of management models in the industrial sector because that is where they originated. With the exception of Osborne and Gaebler (1992), public management reform has been a borrower rather than an originator of reform concepts. That extends to the National Performance Review too. It tends to mimic the private sector's Baldridge criteria concerning what constitutes an excellent organization. It is important to know that, although the genesis of many organizational reforms that express OD values in whole or in part come from business, implementation problems are different in many consequential ways in the government sector.

2

Public Administration and OD

What role has Organizational Development (OD) played in the development of organizational thinking in public administration as a field of study? Further, is the practice of Organizational Development different depending on context? In other words, do OD interventions face dissimilar realities in the public/nonprofit arena than are usually encountered in the business sector?

It is fair to say that organizations of all kinds, public, private, and nonprofit, share common interests in their desire to be effective. Organizations of every kind look for ways to do things better, to produce more, to innovate, and to survive. Organizations are attentive to techniques that address needs for potency and durability.

Although the search for high performance is a generic objective in most organizations, how the strategy plays itself out in various zones cannot not be overlooked. There are differences between public and private organizational operational arenas, and they matter when it comes to Organizational Development.

A note of caution is warranted before drawing hard lines between sectors. All organizations appear to enjoy a certain measure of "publicness" (Bozeman, 1987). The problems of coping with turbulent, changing external environments and aligning internal purposes to those realities is an enduring, usual problem for all organizations. Area distinctions do exist. In the public case, environmental conditions create special challenges for the practice of OD but they are not so powerful that thriving change initiatives cannot be realized. Quite to the contrary, there is evidence that the success rate in public OD is both respectable and encouraging (Golembiewski, 1969, 1985).

Public OD

The central question raised by Organizational Development is whether organizations can promote conditions of work that are developmental and beneficial for both individuals and the organization. This issue is manifest in the study of public administration through its focus on leadership, motivation, group dynamics, communication, participation, decisionmaking, human resources management, principles of management, and organizational theory. Moreover, all of the critical thinking about ideal-type bureaucracy represents core values and assumptions of OD whether or not they are made explicit (e.g., Hummel, 1987).

The study of administration has always had a strong leadership and managerial component and a search for the best way to organize and create conditions for high performance in organizations. The management school is but a single wing of the public administration field but it has always been an important one. The historical tension between managerial reforms of all types and the perceived negative effects of the bureaucratic model has synthesized into the encouragement of more humanistic values in public management. OD is a major countervailing idea to the idealism represented by the rationalist bureaucratic paradigm.

Organizational Development is implicitly and explicitly part of public administration practice. Administrators have to cope with change every day. They have to find ways to involve employee know-how in improving their operations. They wrestle with the issue of shared vision, motivating staff and involving various stakeholders to find common ground on policy matters. They deal constantly with conflict. They are pressed to develop strategic initiatives, set objectives that are acceptable in a political environment, and more and more they are driven to measure performance. As Figure 2.1 demonstrates, OD provides administrators with a wide range of tools to help realize their goals. The range of interventions listed in Figure 2.1 summarize the most progressive thinking in administrative thought for more than fifty years.

FIGURE 2.1   Various Intervention Tools for Facilitating Change

Target Group	Interventions Designed to Improve Effectiveness
Individuals	Life- and career-planning activities Coaching and counseling T-Group (sensitivity training) Education and training to increase skills, knowledge in the areas of technical task needs, relationship skills, process skills, decisionmaking, problem solving, planning, goal-setting skills Grid OD phase 1 Work redesign Gestalt OD Behavior modeling
Dyads/Triads	Process consultation Third-party peacemaking Role negotiation technique Gestalt OD
Teams and Groups	Team building—Task directed—Process directed Gestalt OD Grid OD phase 2 Interdependency exercise Appreciative inquiry Responsibility charting Process consultation Role negotiation Role analysis technique "Startup" team-building activities Education in decisionmaking, problem solving, planning, goal setting in group settings Team MBO Appreciations and concerns exercise Sociotechnical systems (STS) Visioning Quality of work life (QWL) programs Quality circles Force-field analysis Self-managed teams
Intergroup Relations	Intergroup activities—Process directed—Task directed Organizational mirroring Partnering Process consultation Third-party peacemaking at group level Grid OD phase 3 Survey feedback
Total Organization	Sociotechnical systems (STS) Parallel learning structures MBO (participation forms) Cultural analysis Confrontation meetings Visioning Strategic planning/strategic management activities Real-time strategic change Grid OD phases 4, 5, 6 Interdependency exercise Survey feedback Appreciative inquiry Search conferences Quality of work life (QWL) programs Total quality management (TQM) Physical settings Large-scale systems change

SOURCE: *Organizational Development* by French/Bell, copyright 1999. Reprinted by permission of Pearson Education, Inc. Upper Saddle River, N.J., 07488.

Figure 2.1 also points out that public administration has not been an originator of much of the theoretical premises and practical applications of Organizational Development but has been an eager borrower of initiatives seen as useful reforms of administrative practice. The methods used by OD practitioners are universal but the operational terrain is not.

Public OD is a more difficult undertaking. The operational domain of public institutions are structured so that change demands the involvement of multiple actors. Politics, not economics, run the show. Organizations cannot set their own missions or decide "what business we are in." Employees are buffered by powerful civil service and union protections not found in the private sector; the entire business of what goes on in public agencies is simply more public. Although public OD agents may be armed with the same tools as their private counterparts, they may not be used in comparable ways. It is fair to say that, given the territory, the public OD change agent requires superior political skills. Ultimately, that is the essential instrument no matter what type of intervention is employed.

Rainey assembles the most comprehensive coverage of the research findings on public-private distinctions. He develops an extensive catalog of exceptional characteristics of public organizations. Some examples are:

- Absence of economic markets for outputs, reliance on governmental appropriations for financial resources.
- Extensive oversight by legislative, executive, courts, and other agencies.
- Greater political attention from an attentive public and considerable pressure from political groups to influence decisions.
- Greater public scrutiny of administrative decisions. The public sees a "right" to access to information and coverage of events not usual in the private sector.
- Greater ambiguity of goals. (1997, pp. 54–95)

In terms of public management, other idiosyncratic features are found. Some of the more salient include:

- Public managers have less decisionmaking discretion because of a thicket of institutional constraints.
- Public managers have weaker control over subordinates because of civil service tenure realities, a greater degree of unionization in the government sector, and alliances subordinates may establish with outside interests.
- The red tape and other features of ideal-type bureaucracy inhibit action.
- Public managers have less opportunity to develop and control reward and incentive structures than their private counterparts. (Rainey, 1997, pp. 54–95)

In general, the public operating domain is full of external actors and interests that battle over competing values. "Too many cooks" is the common perception of the way things work. Conflicts abound and the environment is truly political, with multiple, ambiguous, and conflicting objectives. Political capital is the coin of the realm. These external environmental forces ultimately seep into the administrative structure of the organization, making leadership and management different in ways that matter for those interested in organizational transformation to any meaningful degree.

Although academics might quarrel over the extent of the problem, it is fair to conclude that managers with innovative administrative intent face a sometimes crushing set of obstacles. Golembiewski examines the public-private differences in 1969 and after 1979. He comes to the same conclusions. The public administrative arena is differentiated by:

1. Legal restrictions
2. Lack of economic incentives and market indicators
3. Multiple access
4. Quasi-governmental action
5. Public scrutiny and suspicion
6. Volatile political/administrative interface
7. Drawing boundaries
8. Diverse interests, values, and incentives

9. Procedural regularity and rigidity
10. Short time frame
11. Weak chains of command
12. Lack of professionalism
13. Complexity of objectives (1985, p. 51)

What this means is that the public environment is a stew of politics, low trust, short-term thinking, competing values, conflicting objectives, and a terrain that does not support transformational leadership. Manifold constraints of the public kind are daunting for internal and external change agents. A few examples are instructive.

Third-Party Peacemaking in Different Worlds

Third-party peacemaking is a common type of OD intervention. It is typically a mediation process where a third party works with interpersonal, intragroup, and intergroup disputes. Conflict is natural in organizations and arises from personality differences, quarrels over ends, means, and scarce resources, and the friction that naturally arises from the myriad interdependencies that marble all organizations.

I was involved in a labor dispute between a major international oil company and a strong AFL-CIO union. The issues were typical for the times. Management wanted to reduce the number of employees and gain greater control over work rules they had negotiated away in previous years. They also wanted to put in new work processes at the local oil refinery. The union, on the other hand, was determined to resist layoffs and was not inclined to give back hard-won work rules. They saw nothing in the new production methods that would benefit them. It was a classic employee-relations confrontation.

To be more exact, it was a classic private labor conflict. It was about economics, ultimately; something that could be measured and counted. Principles were in play certainly, but bottom-line accountability in terms of what things cost was the most dominant concern for both parties— how many jobs, how much money gained or lost, and the engineering mechanics of what new work processes would mean for staffing and safety. On the positive side, at least from the point of view of the mediators, everyone necessary to achieve a settlement was present. The union had to check with their members and the representatives of the plant and their lawyers had "corporate principals" to talk to, but essentially representatives for both sides had real authority to negotiate.

At the risk of standing against open government, the mediators considered it a blessing that no one outside of the parties and the mediators had a right to be in the room. In other words, bargaining wasn't an ongoing press conference. My experience with "sunshine bargaining" in Florida is that bargaining is impaired by being open to outsiders. The parties make speeches instead of negotiating. They are fearful of brainstorming because the process produces concepts that may or may not be serious, but if seen by constituencies in the newspapers present real problems. The parties tend to abandon problem-solving or interest-based approaches (win-win) and go back to traditional, positional, adversarial methods. Private bargaining is easier to handle than public negotiations because it is less public.

The negotiations were typically difficult. Interest-based or "win-win" techniques were employed where groups identified their interests, groups brainstormed ideas, and flip charts were posted that listed "options for mutual gain." Tension and outbursts were displayed on occasion. The parties would be integrative some of the time and regress to positional adversarial bargaining at other times. This is predictable although stressful. At one point the conflict became intense enough that the mediators walked out. Still, in the caucuses people who could make decisions or effectively recommend them were face to face with the mediators. Much of what drove solving problems centered entirely on transaction costs—money and time. If a better idea surfaced, it did not matter where it came from, it was accepted. Management had its principals and so did the union, but that was it. They were kept informed as the negotiations progressed and, since my experience was mainly public sector–oriented, the process was cleaner and more direct. A contract was settled in five days and there was no worry about what the legislature of the city council might feel.

Not long after the oil refinery problem, I was asked to deal with a problem in a municipal government. The local police union had held a news conference and demanded the resignation of the chief of public safety. The city had previously had problems with the union, but this caught them off guard and indicated that the relationship between the officers and the administration had deteriorated to its lowest point. The city manager wanted to put an end to the constant warfare between the parties. My job was to see what I could do to help create conditions of dialogue and restore some sense of teamwork. This was not a problem to be handled through contract negotiations, it was treated as an OD intervention. There was much to overcome.

The fact that a press conference had been held to put the issue on the table is not unusual in the public sector. It would be extraordinary in the private sector; it is unusual for private parties to go public until they have reached an impasse after hard bargaining or have achieved a settlement. In this case, the press conference was the first move to address a series of internal management issues. Although holding a press conference is often effective in getting the attention of higher administration, it automatically escalates issues and spreads the conflict. It raises issues of "face" because it makes it difficult for persons to back away or back down later.

An attempt to force the removal of the chief was a way to get at several underlying issues that can be classified as "unresolved prior conflicts." Making it a public problem immediately transformed the issues into a communitywide political problem that invited more press and communication through the public media. Both sides were chasing votes in an election environment. Council members were loathe to lose police support and were lobbied heavily by everyone with a stake in the outcome. The city manager's job depended on the goodwill of the mayor and the council and he had to play his politics carefully. The community had a natural affection for police personnel and wondered why they felt so strongly that they were not being treated fairly. This kind of situation is not what the private CEO faces when there is an internal administrative problem, even though politics are part of every business operation.

The result of the press conference was to make it impossible for the city manager to fire the chief. The city manager said the chief was made "bulletproof" by the press conference. If the chief were fired as a result of a press conference, then what other demands made in the media would follow? Who knows? Perhaps there would be a press conference to demand the resignation of the city manager. He felt that the union had tied his hands. The city manager was not going to conduct personnel policy through the press. The situation worsened.

The number of complaints grew and made the newspapers on a regular basis. The police union had representatives speak to local service clubs about problems of understaffing and other issues. They filed lawsuits, dragging the courts into the process. They attempted to get the firefighters' union to join them to create a stronger political coalition, but that did not work. The refusal of the fire union to help out led to a bizarre incident: The president of the police union called in a road accident and the fire department responded "Code 3," or came to the scene very fast. The president of the police union felt that the fire equipment had responded too quickly, posing a threat to the safety of the citizens in the community, and tried to arrest two members of the fire department on the spot. Eventually, the firefighters won financial awards from the city because of the actions of the police union president.

I had several meetings with police personnel to work on getting some communication on the problems, but it did not work. Team building failed and so did everything else I tried. The problem had evolved into a public campaign and persons were not inclined to lose any advantage by sitting down and privately working out their issues. I ended up talking with the mayor about the problem and had her support. The editor of the local newspaper talked to me on more than one occasion. A state legislator was involved. So were members of the city council. The problem was undeniably political. Lots of OD problems are political, but in my experience, not quite like this. It is fair to say that this type of situation is not uncommon in government, but it is unusual in the private sector. This case illustrates the real differences between practicing OD in the public versus the private sphere.

Another brief example is enlightening concerning the type of issues faced by OD practitioners in government as opposed to business. I mediated between a library association that wanted full access to a wide range of material and a statewide group convinced that certain materials were pornographic. At one meeting of the library board, a librarian wrapped herself in the American flag to make the point that the other side stood for censorship, which was un-American. She did this right before a member of the opposing group arrived with video equipment to show the board so-called pornographic material, which she believed was un-American. The board declined to look at it. The press was present. The room was packed with supporters of each side. The issues represented deep value conflicts. Dealing with deep public conflict is not like the customary private-sector retreat at a resort with breaks by the lake and golf on the side.

The Public Realities

There is no value consensus in society. From welfare reform to the appropriate mission of correctional facilities on how best to deal with the environment to the best way to reduce teenage pregnancy, Americans disagree. What is good for children, how to stop drug abuse, how to regulate nursing homes, and how to manage wilderness areas are all "wicked issues" and the public sector deals with them all. Changing organizations inevitably must confront what is normative in these policy areas. OD has to help people clarify strategic and mission-related issues. That is difficult when what can be done or what the vision might be is inevitably subject to contentious wrangling outside the control of the people who are trying to build consensus on what ends to pursue and the means to accomplish them.

Organizational change in government faces a messier transformational agenda. There are political players with heavy access everywhere. Everything is more public. If that were not enough, the operating framework of government administration is intentionally structured to be low trust (Carnevale, 1995). Abuse of power is a principal concern so checks and balances are the norm. These can be stifling to innovation, creativity, and change. Although there are calls for high-performance work systems in government, obstacles exist at every turn for the person who wants to alter the status quo. OD in government is an especially artful undertaking.

OD Development and Public Administration

The work of Douglas McGregor (1960), Chris Argyris (1957), Rensis Likert (1961), Frederick Herzberg (1966), Warren Bennis (1969), and

Abraham Maslow (1954, 1962, 1965), among others, challenged conventional thinking about the relationship between individuals and organizations. These "Third Wave" psychologists believed that work should support the growth and development of people and that the governance of work institutions should be more democratic. Collectively, these ideas have been identified by a number of labels, but the most common are "Process Consultation" and "Organization Development" (Harmon and Mayer, 1986).

The Argyris/Simon Exchange

Humanistic writers were especially critical of rational-man theoreticians. The humanists believed rationalists ignored the expressive needs of people at work and supported status quo bureaucracies because of their assumptions that positivist methods were most appropriate when studying organizational behavior. Rationalists were accused of worshiping instrumental rationality because its impersonality made it the correct way to investigate and manage organizations.

In 1973, a confrontation of the two schools appeared in a series of exchanges between Chris Argyris and Herbert Simon in the *Public Administrative Review* (PAR). Argyris opened the debate with an article, "Some Limits of Rational Man Organizational Theory," that spoke of

> new stirrings in public administration that may be seen as part of a broader intellectual debate that has evolved in the field of organizational behavior. Scholars on both sides of the issue are in agreement that it is important to design organizations that are more effective. One side believes that this can be best accomplished through increasing rationality and descriptive research; the other on increasing the humane dimensions and therefore normative research. (1973, p. 253)

That is tame enough, but Argyris extended his argument to accuse the rationalists of supporting "formal pyramidal structures":

> Management was in control, management defined the organization's goals, management defined and assigned tasks, management defined standards, management gave orders, management made men think and

behave as the organization wanted them to behave. It is organizational structures such as these that lead to organizational entropy, ineffective decision making, especially on the important decisions. (1973, p. 255)

Herbert Simon was identified as the most prominent of the rationalists. That invited his response to the allegations. In Simon's article, "Organizational Man: Rational or Self-Actualizing?" the rationalist response was given. Simon wrote:

In Argyris's Dionysian world, reason is one of the shackles of freedom. The rational man is cold, constrained, and incapable of self-actualization and peak "experiences." Man must throw over his reason, must respond to impulse in order to release the swaddled Real Person within.

In my Appolonian world, reason is the handmaiden of freedom and of creativity. It is the instrument that enables me to have peak experiences unimaginable to my cat or my dog. It is the instrument that enables me to dream and design. It is the instrument that enables me and my fellow men to create environments and societies that can satisfy our basic needs, so that all of us—and not just a few—can experience some of the deeper pleasures of sense and mind. And because we depend so heavily upon reasons to create and maintain a humane world we see the need to understand reason better—to construct a test theory of reasoning man. (1973, p. 352)

In the same issue as Simon's response, Argyris called for a reconciliation of sorts by indicating that rationalism and humanism were not mutually exclusive and that "reason for me, is not, and has never been, a shackle of freedom" (1973, p. 356). In a sense, this duel between different perspectives of the nature of man and the appropriate focus of intellectual research was fought out in terms of a false dichotomy where belief in one idea presupposed a lack of caring about the worth of other concepts. In the end Argyris was right about dualistic thinking about the choices involved in trying to comprehend the needs of man, organizations, and society. He understood that theory could transcend and embrace more than two ideas in extreme circumstances.

The debate captured in the Argyris/Simon exchange continues. Its expression is less grand but the points are essentially the same. Organizational Development is seen as "soft" and not contributing to the accomplishment of the goals of the instrumental rationalists, who expect organizations to behave in an idealized, clockwork way. Schwartz describes the clockwork organization:

> ... Everybody knows what the organization is all about and is concerned solely with carrying out its mission; people are basically happy at their work; the level of anxiety is low; people interact with each other in frictionless, mutually supportive cooperation; and if there are any managerial problems at all, these are basically technical problems, easily solved by someone who has the proper skills and knows the correct techniques of management. (1990, p. 7)

Schwartz compares the clockwork organization with the "snake pit" organization:

> Here, everything is always falling apart, and people's main activity is to see that it doesn't fall on them; nobody really knows what is going on, though everyone cares about what is going on because there is danger in not knowing; anxiety and stress are constant companions and people take little pleasure in dealing with each other, doing so primarily to use others for their own purposes or because they cannot avoid being so used themselves. Managerial problems here are experienced as intractable, and mangers feel that they have done well if they are able to make it through the day. (1990, p. 8)

Schwartz uses the familiar public administration case of the space shuttle disaster to make his point: the organizational ideal of perfect clockwork functioning sets serious problems in dealing with reality for organizations and the people who work in them.

These debates illustrate how ideas about humanism versus rationalism have been conducted at the fringes of the theoretical range. Only recently has there been recognition that organizations can be productive in instrumental terms and accomplish such ends through the participation and development of staff. The two sets of values—structure, predictability, technology, and a fair measure of measurement and control—can coexist with concerns about individual development and learning, restoring to staff the concept as well as the execution of tasks and the involvement of staff to gain organizational value from what they know about production, customers, and clients. The persistence of the field of Organizational Development has contributed much to establishing some measure of balance between the dominance of the idealism at the beginning of the last century and the real needs and experiences of people at work. OD has transcended dualism and accommodated both rational and humanistic values.[1]

OD's Place in the History of Public Administration

Discussion of Organizational Development in public administration necessarily leads to the work of two individuals: Robert T. Golembiewski and Neely D. Gardner. Both men brought the values and assumptions of Organizational Development into the study and practice of public administration.

Golembiewski

Like any other field, public administration is defined by the questions it addresses. Golembiewski's *Men, Management, and Morality* (1965) establishes the normative relationship between individuals and organizations and was published about the same time as the work of humanists such as Argyris, Bennis, McGregor, and others. In the book, Golembiewski offers five values that support the idea of the individual freedom of workers:

(1) Work must be psychologically acceptable to the individual. . . .
(2) Work must allow man to develop his own faculties. . . . (3) The work task must allow the individual considerable room for self-determination. . . . (4) The worker must have the possibility of controlling, in a meaningful way, the environment within which the task is to be performed. . . . (5) The organization should not be the sole and final arbiter of behavior; both the organization and the individual must be subject to an external moral order. (1965, p. 65)

These propositions are fully consistent with the three principal values of OD. They are democratic, humanistic, and optimistic about how organizations ought to be managed. Golembiewski doesn't directly attack the strong positivist values of the discipline of public administration, but he insists that organizational forms that suppress individual freedom, growth, and development are in a real sense immoral. He urges the creation of conditions in which organizations can be effective without crushing humanity in the process. In this regard, he may be considered a radical humanist, a paradigm underwritten by concern for freedom of the human spirit (Burrell and Morgan, 1979).

Golembiewski's writing concerning OD is far-reaching. A few of his most notable works include *Renewing Organizations* (1972), *Approaches to Planned Change* (1979), and *Humanizing Public Organizations* (1985), in which he reports that OD interventions in the public sector enjoy a relatively notable success rate. Successes are comparable with those found in the private sector. Others (compare with Robertson and Seneviratne, 1995) support his conclusions. In other work, Golembiewski reports that OD success in the public sector is about the same as in business (Golembieski, Proehl, and Sinck, 1982) or even greater (Golembiewski and Sun, 1990).[2]

In sum, Golembiewski's work constantly raises questions about the human factor in organizational life and what place freedom, democracy, and human development have in public organizations. His research, practice, and theoretical ideas offer compelling evidence that OD has a useful place in the discipline.

Neely Gardner

Gardner is not widely known. He was considered an expert in public service training and spent most of his time working in and around California state government. He was also involved in the National Training and Development Service (NTDS) and employed an action training and research philosophy as a method for changing organizations. His work and ideas are summarized in *Changing Organizations: Practicing Action Training and Research*, written by Raymon Bruce and Sherman Wyman in 1998. Most of the material for the book comes from Gardner's journals.

What makes Gardner notable is that his practice of OD embodied much wisdom in changing organizations. Moreover, he was a public practitioner who was thoroughly engaged in OD practice in major state organizations in one of America's largest state governments.

Gardner employed classic OD as a practitioner. He spurned the idea that change came about from one-shot interventions. He appreciated organizations as complex systems that could not be significantly transformed by intermittent interventions in only some parts and not others. He also held firm that change agents did not "fix" organizations but favored helping staff members learn to create conditions of sustainable innovation on their own. He was a devotee of action research, which is a process that "encourages employees to participate in innovation, fact finding, analysis, problem identification and solving, response strategy development, and evaluation of results" (Bruce and Wyman, 1998, p. 11). Finally, he did not see OD as "soft," but as a solid way to improve organizational performance. Aside from Golembiewski, and admittedly in a different way, Gardner is one of public administration's foremost OD pioneers.

Conclusion

Organizational Development is a values-laden technology used to change organizations. It arises from the Human Relations movement, especially the writings of Argyris, Bennis, McGregor, Lewin, and Likert during the 1960s, although its roots go back to the Hawthorne Studies conducted decades earlier. Much of what is written about OD comes from private-sector experiences. OD ideas found their way into the discipline of public administration mainly through the work of Robert T. Golembiewski. As we shall see in later chapters, the question of the relationship between individuals and organizations is a constant focus of theorists from the public management segment of the field to the present day.

As research on public-private distinctions matured, one of the questions it invited was whether OD traditions in government were different from practices in the business sector. Persuasive evidence exists, first, that the operating context of public organizations is different from the private domain. Second, research shows that public OD faces a set of significant challenges not found in the private sector because of these variations. Third, encouraging data is found that suggests that public OD is as successful, and perhaps realizes slightly more positive outcomes, than private experiences.

Organizational Development is about change. One of the major problems in practicing OD is people's resistance to change, their fear and defensiveness when it is introduced. In the next chapter, I examine why individuals resist change, even when it represents a chance to change their lives and organizations in positive ways.

Notes

1. These kinds of dualistic either/or conceptualizations are singularly part of the Western way of thinking about issues and misses what Eastern thought suggests about the resolution of contradictions and the unity of opposites. The dialectics of Western thinking has value when synthesis occurs and innovation and creativity result. Still, much too much of the conflict in organizations is the inability to comprehend that the truth of the situation is often paradoxical and peace is achieved through transcendent methods that allow seemingly different interests to be integrated.

2. The works cited here by Golembiewski barely scratch the surface of his writings about Organizational Development and public administration. Much more is available to the student of OD in public administration that cannot be done justice here.

3

The Issue of Change

If you want to make enemies, try to change something.
Woodrow Wilson

Organizations cannot change unless individuals change. Generally, people do not like change and will resist it if they can. Conscious and unconscious obstacles block change. Since change is at the heart of Organizational Development (OD), understanding the psychological barriers that obstruct transformation is crucial. Organizational Development is more than process, techniques, and overarching values. It is fundamentally about the human experiencing these things. It is in people's heads that real change occurs, if organizations are to be transformed.

Mind-Sets

People have different cosmologies or worldviews. When any two individuals experience an event, for example, shared perceptions are unlikely. The cognitive mental maps of the observers differ. Images or frames are personal paradigms or models of being, believing, and acting in the world (Morgan, 1997; Bolman and Deal, 1991). They are rich in their diversity.

Another way to characterize how people impose structure, templates, or meaning on a particular domain is captured by the term "schema" or a particular lens used for seeing and understanding

(Quinn and Cameron, 1988). These psychological predispositions color what is attended to, the import attached to events, and how persons behave.

According to Joel Barker (1992, p. 32): A paradigm is a set of rules and regulations (written or unwritten) that does two things: it establishes or defines boundaries and it tells you how to behave inside the boundaries in order to be successful.

There is nothing inherently wrong with having certain anticipations concerning events. Paradigms provide limits and structure in our lives, reflect our values, help us make sense of things, and establish necessary confines. Without them, existence would be chaos. The problem with deeply held beliefs, however, is that they sometimes blind us to the need for change. Our paradigms are filters that permit only certain things in at the same time they keep other perspectives out. The problem is that what is screened may be the critical data or feedback we need to pay attention to, if we want to cope successfully with our environment. Schemata establish the proverbial "boxes" consultants constantly encourage staff to transcend. To the OD practitioner, mind-sets are issues of tremendous importance. They establish the degree of resistance to change.

The Process of Change: The Issue of Resistance

The Ladder of Inference

People do not like to be wrong. Senge and associates (1994, pp. 242–246) focus on how mind-sets make people feel they are right about things, and therefore are unwilling to alter beliefs. Individuals fall into a trap where their beliefs are the truth, the truth is obvious, their viewpoints are based on real data, and the data selected is the relevant data. A seamless circuit is created that is self-reinforcing and feels right even when it reflects only a partial and often distorted view of existence.

Senge and associates (1994) developed a "ladder of inference" that illustrates the pathway to self-sealing awareness (see Figure 3.1). People's perceptions are selective; they see what they need to see,

FIGURE 3.1   How People Shape Reality

The Ladder of Inference

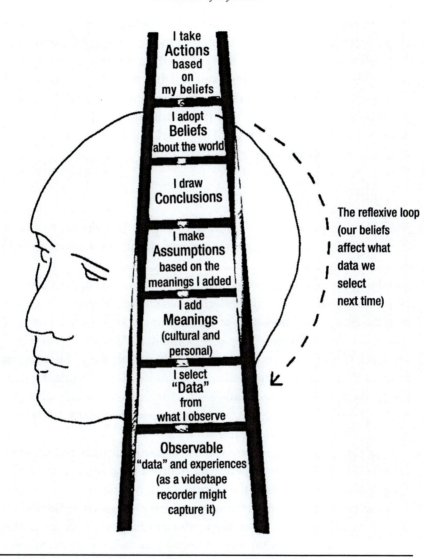

I take
Actions
based
on
my beliefs

I adopt
Beliefs
about the world

I draw
Conclusions

I make
Assumptions
based on the
meanings I added

I add
Meanings
(cultural and
personal)

I select
"Data"
from
what I observe

Observable
"data" and experiences
(as a videotape
recorder might
capture it)

The reflexive loop
(our beliefs
affect what
data we
select
next time)

SOURCE: From *The Fifth Discipline Fieldbook* by Peter Senge, Charlotte Roberts, et al., copyright 1994 by Peter Senge, Art Kleiner, Charlotte Roberts, Richard B. Ross, and Bryan J. Smith. Used by permission of Doubleday, a division of Random House.

which is usually what agrees with their preconceptions. People gather information and attach meaning that supports what they want to see and hear. They make assumptions on the faulty data and then draw conclusions they think are based on a powerful rationality. They adopt beliefs based on their delusions and then act as if there were no other interpretation of what is right. Getting people to climb down the ladder and to open themselves to other notions is a formidable undertaking. Even when persons come to some awareness that they might be wrong, they won't admit it, fearing loss of face. Shame and blame is such an unhappy part of our work culture that persons learn to cover mistakes and to resist looking wrong.

The Organizational Iceberg

When thinking about organizational change it is common to use the idea of an iceberg to make several points about the issue of transformation. This example is another good way to understand how difficult changing people and organizations can be. The superstructure of the iceberg exists above the waterline, visible to the eye. It is observable; the physical dimensions of the setting are known and easily understood (Gibson, Ivancevich, and Donnelly, 2000, p. 454; see Figure 3.2). Considerable information is easily obtainable from the organizational superstructure: budget documents, job descriptions, strategic plans, charts of the organization's structure, mission statements, personnel policies and practices, and measures of productivity and efficiency. This is the formal organization.

Most change-related information in organizations is not apparent on the surface. Like an iceberg, the reality of the organization runs deep and is unseen. This is the informal organization.

Organizational climates, or how people really feel, lie below the surface of organizations. Unresolved prior conflicts exist in the netherworld and inter- and intragroup rivalries lurk in the deep. Degrees of trust, like thermal planes, fluctuate below. Assorted personalities compete below the outer surface. Politics and power engage in the subterranean. This is the bottom area where rumors flourish, the home of private disagreements that underlie the public consensus that appears outwardly. This is where attitudes, emotions, and real feelings are

FIGURE 3.2 Looking Below the Waterline

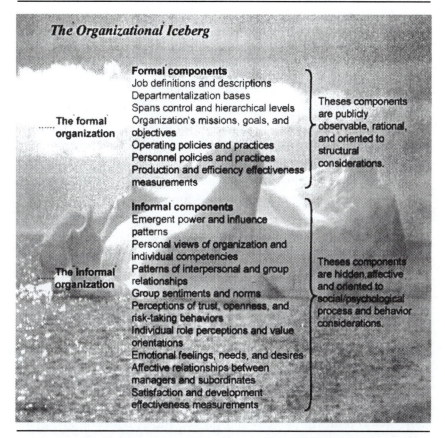

The Organizational Iceberg

The formal organization

Formal components
Job definitions and descriptions
Departmentalization bases
Spans control and hierarchical levels
Organization's missions, goals, and objectives
Operating policies and practices
Personnel policies and practices
Production and efficiency effectiveness measurements

Theses components are publicly observable, rational, and oriented to structural considerations.

The informal organization

Informal components
Emergent power and influence patterns
Personal views of organization and individual competencies
Patterns of interpersonal and group relationships
Group sentiments and norms
Perceptions of trust, openness, and risk-taking behaviors
Individual role perceptions and value orientations
Emotional feelings, needs, and desires
Affective relationships between managers and subordinates
Satisfaction and development effectiveness measurements

Theses components are hidden, affective and oriented to social/psychological process and behavior considerations.

SOURCE: Reprinted with permission from *Organizations* (2000) James L. Gibson, John M. Ivancevich, and James H. Donnelly Jr., p. 454, by McGraw-Hill.

submerged and repressed, where socio/psychological issues abound. This is where the OD change agent must plunge.

It is useful to remember that organizations don't change unless people do and humans display a public persona that is unlikely to be the real self. Behind the public mask lies the real person. Reaching the private self, peeling away his or her defenses, and getting to the deeper issues is crucial as a prerequisite for organizational change. The goal is to open persons and organizations to greater potential.

The Four-Room Apartment

Change involves going through a multistep process. It is a journey. Weisbord (1987) illustrates the steps through the conception of a "Four-Room Apartment" (see Figure 3.3).[1] This is a place where people live through their choices about change.

The first room is "Contentment," or general satisfaction with the status quo. It is fair to say that people and organizations are rarely, if ever, in the position where everything is going just right. But there are occasions when most consequential matters are reasonably well in hand and a feeling of general satisfaction is warranted. In this turbulent world, both for persons and organizations, contentment is difficult to sustain.

The second room is "Denial." What naturally happens in personal and organizational life is that what is wanted and expected are not always attainable. Negative feedback is received that suggests that something is awry. The feedback can be subtle or arise from extreme stress or a sense of crisis. This focal event triggers a push away from the idea that all is well (Heatherton and Nichols, 1994). The individual's brain experiences a sense of cognitive dissonance, that the anticipated is not realized (Festinger, 1957).

One reaction to the disruption generated by negative feedback is to investigate the threatening data, confront its meaning, and do what is necessary. The other choice, and the one that leads to resistance and defensive conduct in persons and organizations, is to employ an array of psychological barricades to deny the menacing reality.

There are several things that the unconscious does to protect itself from hostile information.

- Repression   "Bury" it.
- Denial   Refuse to acknowledge it.
- Projection   Blame someone or something else for the bad feelings.
- Rationalization   Explain it away as anomalous.
- Idealization   Play up the good aspects of the situation.

These reactions to discordant knowledge by individuals are similar to symptoms of Groupthink (Janis, 1972). Comparable pathologies

FIGURE 3.3   The Four-Room Apartment and Individual Change

THE PROCESS OF CHANGE

SOURCE: Marvin Weisbord, *Productive Workplaces: Organizing and Managing for Dignity, Meaning, and Community* (1987). Reprinted by permission of Jossey-Bass, a subsidiary of John Wiley and Sons.

exist when groups are confronted with information that threatens their psychological safety. In other words, group security is delusional. The signs of Groupthink include:

- An illusion of invulnerability.
- Rationalizations of warnings.
- Exaggerated sense of morality or being right.

- Mind guards emerge to ensure that there is no deviant thinking in the group.
- Competitors are stereotyped as evil.
- Silence is considered agreement. (Janis, 1972, 197–198)

These reactions represent fleeing from the truth, refutation that something is amiss, and unwillingness to alter one's cognitive mental map.

The dynamics of change and denial are also represented in the first stage of Kurt Lewin's (in Schein, 1987) classic model of the change process that proposes three stages of transformation: *unfreezing, changing through cognitive restructuring,* and *refreezing.*

Unfreezing involves the process of "disconfirmation," which is another way of saying that a person's expectations are disappointed. Guilt or anxiety lead the person to try to restore a sense of psychological safety. As discussed previously, the person can choose to face up to the need for change or use a number of psychological defenses to deny the truth of the situation.

The OD practitioner plays a role in the disconfirming process but has to be empathetic with the feelings of the person(s) who have to make the changes. The OD practitioner cannot be threatening and cannot push people too far too fast. Like the therapeutic encounter, clients get the time they need to gain insight that something is wrong and they can do a lot about it. Opening people to change is pure artistry in the practice of OD. It involves a subtle form of agitation through assertiveness and active listening.

The third situation in the Four-Room Apartment process is "Confusion," which is the difficult part of the process. It involves being in the world without a map, experiencing the new. This is the "heroic act" (Quinn, 1996) of refusing to deny the truth and making necessary changes even though there is no guarantee they will work. Joseph Campbell (1973), like Quinn (1996), sees going into the unknown as "the journey of the hero" where the dragon of fear is destroyed. In common mythological stories throughout the world, heroes are people who go out to face the mysterious, hoping to create a better world for themselves and others. In doing so, they must confront the internal dragon of their fears.

As a practicing mediator, it is my goal to take people from denial to the room of confusion. Once I have them cut loose from their psychological barricades and strong positional belief, they are without a map. Disoriented, they are more likely to look for help and to open themselves to other ideas. On more than one occasion I have smiled inwardly, knowing that the people working with me had crossed the line from denial into an unmarked place on their internal maps.

A fairy tale can be instructive. Like Dorothy in the classic film *The Wizard of Oz*, troubled people just want to go home, which means they want a safe state of mind. They are learning, just like Dorothy did, that they have the power to seize control of their lives if they are willing to face the challenges of the journey to renewal. Challenges stand in their way and the consultant, like the Wizard, is not the answer. The solution comes from the people themselves. Their willingness to venture out is a heroic act. As they leave the familiar, they will confront problems and hear threats. They will be exposed to humiliation and will fail at some things. But if they choose to continue the quest they can overcome the demons, fears, witches, and dragons that have held them back. There is always help. A more developed, competent, and confident self emerges. It is the hero's boon. The journey of Dorothy and her friends (each companion an extension of her own fears) has wide application in organizations, much more than a fairy tale might suggest at first glance.

Quinn (1996) admonishes would-be OD practitioners that they cannot change organizations if they cannot change themselves. He claims that change agents have no right to ask people to take risks with their lives, if the change agents themselves have not had the courage to make changes in their own existence. According to Quinn, change agents have an ethical obligation to have more in their OD repertoire than a bunch of abstractions that encourage others to take risks when they are unwilling to model the same actions in their own lives. They too must be willing to "walk naked into the land of uncertainty" (1996, p. 10) or "get lost with confidence" (1996, p. 11).

Other OD scholars formulate the same set of values. Schein explains that the second step of Lewin's change model is a process of cognitive restructuring where the goal is "helping the client see things, judge things, feel things, and react to things differently based on a new point of view" (1987, p. 93). This is also consistent with French and Bell's description of a normative reeducative strategy of change (1999, pp. 95–97). This line of attack recognizes that norms are the basis for behavior and change; old norms are discarded and new ones are embraced. Of course, this is more easily depicted in theory than accomplished in practice. Nonetheless, change is learning and learning is change.

Change means letting go of the comfortable. It is based on the belief that beating the fear will produce better results. There is no shortcut to renewal or refreezing. A price always has to be paid. Even when people and systems are restabilized, it is not likely to be long-lasting. In the timeless statement attributed to Heraclitus, "There is nothing more permanent than change."

So why don't people and organizations change? They are afraid. Campbell (1973) equates the fear of change as a dragon to be slayed before moving from the darkness to the light of renewal. It is confronting the fear in oneself that is the heroic act. The idea that heroes are not afraid is misplaced. When my students are asked why change is so difficult in their personal and work lives, they invariably respond in one of the following ways:

1. It is better to live with the pain you know than to take a chance on something you don't know.
2. There is no assurance that change will bring success.
3. People will judge you in lesser terms, if you try something new and fail.
4. Waiting for the threat to go away sometimes works.
5. Leaders are most responsible for problems and if the leaders will leave, and they often do, a new leader might make things better.
6. The problem is other people and when they change things will be all right.
7. People will not like or accept me if I start changing things.
8. I have carefully built my career and no one is coming in here and changing things so that I lose all the investments I've made to get ahead.

9. This is just the latest "flavor-of-the-month" change initiative anyway and they come and go without any result other than churning the organization and achieving nothing.

It is rational for people to resist change. According to Kets de Vries and Insead, relying on Freud (1920):

There are forces within each individual that oppose change. Social and psychological investments in the status quo make it very difficult to weaken that opposition. Anxiety associated with the uncertainty of engaging in something new or becoming once again exposed to old dangers and risks, for example, often prompts people to resist change. In an effort to reduce such anxiety, people allow avoidance behaviors—those means by which we keep ourselves out of frightening situations—to become deeply ingrained. Furthermore, repetition compulsions—the inclination to repeat past behavior despite the suffering attached to that behavior—is an all too human tendency. (1999, p. 646)

Leading Change

The leadership model with the greatest currency these days is the transformational type. It is written about by numbers of authors, but the heart of the model is that leadership is about encouraging change, sharing common vision, communicating effectively, modeling behavior, encouraging teamwork, being credible, trustworthy, and, especially, empowering, or enabling others to act. Charisma, intellectual stimulation of followers, and individualized consideration are also consequential (Burns, 1978; Bass, 1985; Conger and Kanungo, 1987; Bennis and Nanus, 1985). The model has much to recommend it but sometimes the rhetoric outruns reality.

Recently in one of my classes, students were asked to list the characteristics of great leadership and post them on flip charts. Not one group used the word "empowerment." I asked why. They said they were sick of the "e-word." It was a lie in their experience. Their leaders had learned new language at seminars but had not altered how they actually behaved. The students had been changed and reformed to death. They felt preyed upon. Perhaps they were sick of the "management drivel in all spheres" so evident in the following:

> The new authority will be: member led, officer driven, customer focused; a team environment where the whole is greater than the sum of its parts; a flat management structure where employees and mangers are fully empowered and decisions are devolved close to the customer; a culture of learning rather than blame; a clear sense of direction and purpose. A firm commitment to delivery of high quality public services through a combination of direct-provision and effective partnerships. (Micklethwait and Wooldridge, 1996, p. 1)

This boilerplate rhetoric is laughable, if it weren't so commonly attached to many organizational change interventions. Certainly, there are numerous instances of sincerely led conversions. Some organizations stick to the agenda and truly engage employees in framing the nature of change. They give power to staff by recognizing what they know and the value of their experiences. Knowledge is only power when power decides, and not the other way around. There are stories of positive change interventions. Still, the quick-fix artists have encouraged a rising cynicism about organizational reform and it sabotages OD work everywhere (Shapiro, 1995).

Rainey adds another impediment to change that is peculiar to the public sector. He suggests that some so-called good government types encourage "ephemeral, rhetorical, symbolic, misdirected, half-hearted, disingenuous, and faddish changes and reforms" (1999, p. 139). Situations exist where too many reforms are tried with insufficient planning and precious little patience. This leads to the growing cynicism among staff about the latest program to save their world. Not all reformers have good intentions. These characters play games by talking about change in government without caring if innovations are actually produced. They want to use the rhetoric of reform to build political capital for themselves or as an excuse to cut government or just fire employees. According to Rainey, these "reformers" are just mouthing old-fashioned antistate ideologies and have no real commitment to make better an institution they really abhor. The rhetoric is cover for a kind of antigovernment political correctness and is destructive in its results. Given the hypocrisy, perhaps some change failures in government are self-fulfilling; employees who do the work recognize insincerity when they see it and are worn down by committing to the lie that organizational leaders care about them and what they do. The rational response is resistance based on rational mistrust.

The Continuum of Resistance to Change

There is a spectrum or continuum of possible reactions to change. These can range from acceptance to deliberate sabotage, depending on the extent that people feel their needs are being frustrated. Often refusal to change suggests an unwillingness to become motivated in a positive direction. Opposition to change can be an entirely different form of physics. It doesn't run away, it attacks. Arnold S. Judson (1991, p. 1948) provides a useful model of the range of responses to change that works as follows (see Figure 3.4).

The range of reactions to change is considerable. Some responses are passive whereas others are aggressive. Change involves feelings of mourning and loss, privation, and separation. These emotions always make organizational change problematic and, at some level, encourage strong defensive conduct.

One of my students is an assistant warden at a faith-based women's prison in the Southwest. Part of the inmates' rehabilitation involves dealing with the issue of chemical dependency, which is one of the prevalent causes for the incarceration of women. A court case was decided that suggested that the classic twelve-step program used to help alcoholics and a host of other addictive disorders was too religious in nature and could not be employed without modification in a public correctional facility. It was the assistant warden's job to change the chemical dependency therapy to conform to the idea that it must not be administered based on a specific type of theology.

It is not surprising that a number of counselors held strong religious values that they saw as crucial to rehabilitate inmates. To them, to compromise the presence of traditional faith-based ideas was to

52

FIGURE 3.4   How People React to Change

This resistance may take many forms. The particular form depends on the individual's personality, on the nature of the change itself, on attitudes toward it and on forces deriving from the group and from the organization and its environmental context. Whatever the form of resistance, all types of opposition are a kind of aggressive or hostile behavior.

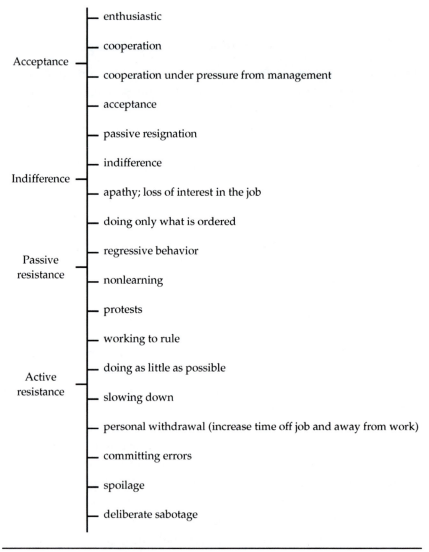

Acceptance
— enthusiastic
— cooperation
— cooperation under pressure from management
— acceptance

Indifference
— passive resignation
— indifference
— apathy; loss of interest in the job
— doing only what is ordered

Passive resistance
— regressive behavior
— nonlearning
— protests

Active resistance
— working to rule
— doing as little as possible
— slowing down
— personal withdrawal (increase time off job and away from work)
— committing errors
— spoilage
— deliberate sabotage

SOURCE: Judson, A. 1991. *Changing Behavior in Organizations: Minimizing Resistance to Change.* Cambridge, MA: Basil Blackwell, Inc.

destroy the therapy and admit witchcraft into the institution. This case is an ideal example of the confrontation between change and the needs of individuals. It sharply depicts the intensity of resistance that can occur when one threatens the deepest held values and beliefs of people about the very meaning of existence.

The assistant warden encountered some quiet acceptance among some of the staff but active resistance and sabotage by others. She involved the staff in making the transition from the traditional model to a new one where spirituality was welcomed as long as it was not traditional. Traditionalists were not prevented from prayer or attending church, whether they were staff or inmates. Still, the traditionalists among the staff perceived the assistant warden as an agent of the devil. They refused to express their feelings in most of the meetings where staff could brainstorm about problems and solutions and went so far as to agitate some inmates and subvert necessary reports to the state department of corrections, which had oversight responsibility to ensure that the changes were made.

In the best tradition of OD, participation and listening to the voice of employees was paramount. Still, aggressive resistance continued in some quarters. High involvement was insufficient. The assistant warden fired some employees and had some inmates transferred. She was resolute in getting the job done. For those who believe that all problems can be facilitated endlessly, this case demonstrates that sometimes people are the problem and if they cannot make changes or work with other staff to improve the transformations under consideration, they have to go. The case points out how deeply value conflicts can run. It reveals how the entire range of resistances to change can manifest in a single case. It suggests that there are types of conflict that pit an individual's beliefs against the goals of an organization so severely that a reasonable measure of collaboration is not possible. These are the toughest cases of all.

Passive-aggressive behavior is a common psychological response to unwanted change. In one union situation I faced, the union was losing its fight to prevent alterations in work rules. The union had the right to strike but knew they would be replaced if they tried. So they decided to stay on the job and make life miserable for the company, carefully following the letter but not the spirit of the new rules. Moreover, they swore to "slow drag" the customers. In other words, employees would respond to service calls in a manner devoid of enthusiasm. The moral is that people will find a way to interfere with what they don't believe in. If change is so difficult, then how do some people accomplish it?

Encouraging Change Through PC

Organizational Development values process. Process Consultation (PC), or how things are done, is sometimes as important to OD practitioners as what is done (Schein, 1987, 1988). PC is similar to the assumptions found in much counseling and therapy where clients are allowed to be directly involved in solving their problems and figuring out what is wrong and what action might be tried to correct them. The OD change agent is a "helper," not a "fixer." Change is not imposed on the client and the client is not told what to do. The need for change is a matter of insight by the client. This self-discovery process is facilitated by the organizational therapist (OD change agent) through a process that shows "unconditional positive regard" for the ideas of the client system about what is wrong and how to fix it (compare with Rogers, 1951).

One of the most important core values in OD is to have a democratic attitude. That means that people have the right to participate and to be involved in working through problems. In an all-too-familiar routine, a survey appears, findings are delivered to the chief administrative officer, and results either disappear or top-down directives materialize that must be followed or else. The people who filled out the survey do not see the results, let alone interpret them. They are not privy to the advice of the internal or external consultant. They do not contribute to any planning. They are drained of information for other people's purposes. This autocratic, outside-in approach is known as the "doctor's mandate" method, where a consultant is engaged, takes the baby's temperature, prescribes medication, and departs while the parents administer the potion to the children. OD doesn't see employees as children. It supports the notion that workers are adults and need to be treated that way (Argyris, 1957). Therefore, democratic processes dominate OD interventions of every kind.

People are more committed to solutions they develop themselves.[2] This idea originates with Carl Rogers (1951, 1969) who stressed the importance of involvement as a way to increase "ownership" of change. PC lets people identify problems and develop plans of action. In the process, they learn how to communicate, trust, and profit from what others contribute. In a group setting, the assembly itself provides a measure of security and support for change. In groups involved in PC, communication means listening as much as talking. Feelings can be expressed, information is shared, and decisions are made by consensus. Synergy, or the idea that the whole is more than the sum of its parts, is possible. Ultimately, PC makes for better quality decisions and opportunities for creativity and growth.

PC is facilitated group problem solving. These group processes range from the very small to the very large.[3] In writing about Large Group Interaction Methods (LGIMs), Bryson and Anderson indicate that they:

> (1) are fast, compared with alternative approaches; (2) build buy-in and commitment from participants; (3) use dissatisfaction as a resource to prompt action on pressing issues or problems; (4) prompt participants to draw on their wisdom and experience, successes and failures; (5) tap participants' collective brain power, increasing the amount of intelligence brought to bear on an issue or problem; (6) get planners, implementers, and other stakeholders—in some cases, the whole system—in the same place to address the same issue or problem; and (7) help to build coalitions for politically feasible change. (2000, p. 144)

LGIMs have come to be used a lot, for example, in communities as ways to talk about the quality of local education or problems associated with growth. They can be used to facilitate large groups interested in a certain statewide policy problem. For instance, in one state various Hispanic groups came together to work on policy issues that affected their constituencies. The League of Women Voters in Oklahoma hold annual "talking circles" throughout several communities to try to build consensus on what should be done statewide concerning the needs of children or the direction taken by the state's correction system. No matter what the use and no matter what the magnitude,

LGIMs have their lineage grounded in the small group work started by Lewin (1947), Bion (1961), and other Organizational Development pioneers who engaged in group training and research. The same values are at work.

PC in the Organization

PC interventions in organizations pay attention to how an organization communicates, shares leadership, permits the expression of feelings, encourages trust, and whether interactions spur creativity and growth. In truth, organizations don't do these things. People do. More specifically, groups do. In a typical situation, PC monitors how individuals actually do things in groups. The guiding idea is that how things are done can be as important as what is accomplished.[4]

One of my cases that involved the leadership of the security division of a major federal agency illustrates the importance of process. The idea was to give agency leaders from throughout the world an opportunity to confront Washington, D.C., authorities on how they felt about current operations and to offer suggestions to improve them. Surveys had been conducted by the agency's human resources department to try to get a handle on sentiments in the field. A face-to-face meeting had already occurred in San Antonio, Texas, but had not gone well, according to most reports. This intervention was another attempt to get the group to process their issues and to come up with ideas for change. Two challenges were evident: to get the group to work together in a reasonably collaborative way and to have the effort produce ideas on how to improve agency performance.

An important issue in OD work is trust. Trust is a highly differentiated attitude that means "faith or confidence in the intentions and actions of a group to be ethical, fair, and non-threatening concerning the rights and interests of others in social exchange relationships" (Carnevale, 1988, 1995). In this case, there was little trust between field and headquarters personnel. That is not an unusual situation, but this time it had been exacerbated by the fact that the field staff felt not listened to and their ideas not cared about. The fact that the agency director had decided to participate in the group's work was encouraging, although risky. Having the boss in the room can be a mixed blessing. Having representatives of the human resources department involved in the process was also tricky. They had been used to getting sentiment from the field and translating that into actions they took to higher authorities for approval. How they felt about really listening to opinions and shaping action from the ground up was worrysome.

The groups worked over three days and opened up. When asked what they wanted from management, they indicated fairness, integrity, greater ethical conduct, more flexibility, improved communications, and "walking the talk," or making the vision meaningful by modeling the behavior that was supposed to be normative for the agency. There were further complaints about a need for more loyalty, coaching and development of staff, treating employees as adults, and, generally, more "trustworthy" behavior. To the credit of the managers present, they participated, pushed critics hard with fair questions, and listened. They did not use their power to shut off or shut down the dialogue. These are difficult topics. There is nothing soft about them. There was a fair amount of conflict evident, although not all of it was directed at upper management. People from different parts of the country did not see things the same way all the time. The conflict was functional and productive.

The work was accomplished in small groups brainstorming ideas onto flip charts that were posted and evaluated in detail. Themes were identified and prioritized. Tentative actions were specified. Facilitators watched as the groups changed. The teams got better at processing the questions. They became more open. There was more participation by more people. Conflict was worked through and humor began to surface time and again. People with differences were able to tease one another. Individuals enjoyed going out to dinner together and talking every night. The field team was being created. The idea that involving people in solving their problems was working. Individuals know what is wrong in their work systems and have the commitment to do something about it, given a chance. The first problem, getting the group to collaborate, was succeeding.

As the retreat ended, the groups decided that instead of taking their results to the general director of the agency, it would be better to take the process they had learned home and replicate it there. In other words, they would give their colleagues and subordinates a chance to experience what they had. Then, when all the regions had processed the concerns, a meeting could be held in the nation's capital that was truly representative of the questions that needed to be addressed. Moreover, a greater sense of community would be created bottom-up in the organization. The group left optimistic and encouraged by what might be possible after all.

Then it all stopped. Once the administrative personnel returned to Washington they decided that it would be too expensive to bring people in to meet the director. Human Resources could pick up the problem. The meeting was useful, but budget pressures and the fact that a good deal of data had surfaced were sufficient to make progress possible. It was classic. "We want your ideas" and "We really want to know how you feel" is a common organizational refrain these days. It works until ideas and feelings fail to fit the administrative model of the day or threaten the turf of certain units high up in the hierarchy. Leadership stepped on the conversation and their espoused theories and their actions did not fit. The outcomes are predictable. People feel betrayed, trust is damaged, rhetoric about shared vision sounds hollow. To go to the heart of the matter, when people are open and involved in the process of change, pulling the rug out from underneath them has nothing but negative consequences. This case did not have a happy ending but it is not atypical.

A story with a better outcome is one where I was asked to work with the Senate staff in a southwestern state in a team-building exercise. The director of the group had attended a Harvard University leadership program and returned full of enthusiasm for involving his staff in creating as good a group as possible. He thought the problems in the group, or the barriers to high performance, would be the usual suspects, such as a need for training or how to deal with the numerous political actors who were sometimes helpful but often obstructionist in getting good legislation drafted. Some structural issues were on the table as well as complaints about communication. It became apparent that many members of the group harbored resentment toward the leader for assorted reasons. Ultimately, those emotions came out, and not gently. I had one of those change agent moments when I wondered if the process would continue or if I had spent my last day working with the group. To the leader's great credit, he heard what was said and really listened to the reality that he had to make changes as a part of the group's overall transformation. He accepted the feedback and got to work in helping to build a strong team. I mention this story to make the point that, although some people cannot handle the data, others will. Some people mean it when they talk about "us" and getting better together. Others are stuck in denial, fixed in their mental maps, and unable to understand that their truth is not the only reality. Experienced change agents contend with both types.

Conclusion

Organizational Development is ultimately about people, not techniques, not intervention methods, not just values and assumptions, although these are all consequential matters. The core problem in successful OD is getting people to take the step into the uncertain world of change where there are no guarantees of success. People think they are rational. They believe they are right about much that goes on in their personal lives and their organizational experiences. The truth is more complex in most cases. Fears, biases, feelings, emotions, stereotypes, selective perception, and all manner of noise distorts and represses what is real and what is possible. People have a right to fear and to the interpretation of their experiences. That must be respected. It is not a crime for staff to find their own meanings and to set individual courses of self-development.

Organizations and people are always in the process of becoming. What is achieved in terms of common purpose in organizations depends very much on the OD change agent. The OD practitioner is in a "helping" role, empathetic always, and an encourager of learning new things and fresh ways to do things. To be successful, OD professionals begin with the people. And they begin with the people where they find them, where they are, with their fears, frames, and images of a world that often appears threatening.

It is important to note what this chapter does not say. It is not preoccupied with whether bureaucracies have peculiar characteristics that make them more difficult to change than other structural forms. Ultimately, it is people who choose to change. There are cases of bureaucratic organizations in state governments that are high performing despite the same political actors, budget constraints, personnel rules, and stakeholder expectations. Other state bureaucracies are stuck in mediocrity. The difference is that in effective organizations people are constructively engaged. They have chosen to do better. They overcome obstacles. They beat the fear. That is why there is no discussion of changing organizations without dealing with the threshold issue of individual willingness to trust, take risk, and step out into the unknown for their own good and for the good of their organizations. It is the characteristics of people that matters the most, not the type of structures they labor in.

Notes

1. Weisbord develops the model from work by C. Janssen in *Personalig Dialektik*, 2d ed. Stockholm: Liber, 1982.

2. A full treatment of group processes in organizations and their influence on individual, group, and organizational learning will be developed in the following chapter.

3. In a later chapter, there will be an extensive discussion of Large Group Interaction Methods as an idea used, not just for organizational change, but also for the development of community consensus on how to solve pressing problems. At this point, it is sufficient to detail the principles of the process and demonstrate how they are fully consistent with OD values and assumptions of the kind embodied in PC.

4. The tools for group processing usually include tables for small groups to gather, flip charts or some other writing material, colored markers, and at least one facilitator. The groups are usually asked a series of questions, brainstorm ideas, search for consensus, and then report their results. These become the material that the room builds on to begin a series of iterative processes until some action strategy is developed. This is at the heart of Action Research and the core technology of OD, which will be discussed in detail in the next chapter.

4

Learning, Power, and Action Research

Knowledge is power.
Francis Bacon

He who has the bigger stick has the better
chance of imposing his definitions of reality.
Peter Berger and Thomas Luckman

Growth involves learning new things and unlearning others. This is the core of the normative reeducative idea that is central to Organizational Development (OD). Involving employees in structured problem solving, allowing them effective voice, and respecting their know-how are the core elements in the physics of learning. Letting people take part encourages sharing ideas, makes synergistic interaction possible, and results in creativity. Participatory learning helps people get rid of distorted thinking, rigid mind-sets, and unrealistic assumptions about other people and problems.

Rather than repress what people know, OD is a champion of participation and staff voice. Supporting every organizational reform movement is the inspiration that getting people involved brings intelligence to the surface and makes learning possible.

Human capital is the combination of knowledge, skills, and abilities possessed by a workforce. It is now widely recognized that human capital is key to high performance in organizations. Organizational theorists and their management counterparts did not always see things this way. They thought that what people knew was important. However, what personnel should know came as a result of top-down rationalistic analysis, standard operating procedures, and driving out variance in how tasks were performed. Knowledge elites ruled. Participation and learning were tightly controlled. What management demanded was doing a job one best way. Variance in task performance was unwelcome. Condoning employee judgment cost money in a world of standardized products and methods of producing them. Knowledge was engineered and did not take account of actual working experience. Employee know-how was systematically devalued.

The idea that labor was a cost, not an asset, is an outgrowth of early thinking in classical economics. The controlling concept was that land, capital, and raw materials were key to productive success in nations. Following World War II, this view began to shift with the emergence of quantitative economics. Traditional economic thinking was unable to explain the dramatic rise in American national income that far exceeded the usual factors that classical economists used to predict levels of productivity in countries. In a speech before the American Economic Association in 1960, Theodore Schultz offered an answer to the question of why America was outproducing what its natural resources would predict as its upward limits. Schultz concluded that the knowledge, skills, and abilities—a nation's intellectual or human capital—enabled a country to transcend the ceiling of what the conventional inputs to productivity could explain. The idea was introduced that, in the modern age, human capital was a benefit and the critical technology at work (Salamon, 1991).

Nowadays it is appreciated that approximately 60 percent of the competitive advantage in organizations comes from advances in worker intelligence (A. P. Carnevale, 1991). In the past, about 80 percent of all jobs involved following standard rules and operating procedures and only 20 percent of occupations required the exercise of significant judgment. Today those proportions are exactly the reverse (Watkins and Marsick, 1993); the old assumptions about human capital no longer hold true in the face of these new realities.

The motivation for a new perspective on human capital is not "soft." The reason for employee involvement is because the instrumental purposes of organizations are well served when people move toward their full working and personal potential. Employee development is mutually beneficial for staff and management. Workforce intelligence, learning capacity, and overall competence that arises from learning is what makes organizations able to cope and to be resilient in a highly competitive world.

The human capital advantage lies beneath the wide array of interventions that characterize OD practice. For instance, confrontation meetings, visioning exercises, search conferences, strategic management activities, quality circles, team building, Total Quality Management (TQM), and comprehensive system change designs all aim to get at what people know and how they feel about organizational problems and potential solutions. Deep change requires people to get in touch with what they know and how they feel and then be allowed to express that as part of the overall change endeavor. OD interventions reveal information outside the experience of organizational authorities. Sharing ideas puts more knowledge into play. The interaction between different forms of knowledge creates tension that may be constructively used for individual and organizational growth.[1]

The practical problem is how to release the power of experiential learning that is latent in the human resources of organizations. There is no change unless workers are willing to share what they experience. There is no action without views of alternative futures. There are no ideas if people are not permitted to be involved. The consequences of denying staff a reasonable measure of agency are severe. According to Senge, "organizations learn only through individuals who learn. Individual learning does not guarantee organizational learning. But without it no organizational learning occurs" (1990, p. 139).

Forces exist that block the release of staff intelligence. Workers resist change and are deeply reluctant to open up about what they know and feel at work. As I already discussed, fear is widespread on the job. That problem is demanding but workable. At least the change agent has the organization in the room. There is, however, a more difficult threshold issue blocking the emancipation of employee ideas: It is antecedent to employee defensiveness. The most challenging impediment to triggering the change process is organizational authorities opposed to sanctioning staff development. Some managers sincerely believe that permitting employees the discretion to identify problems and develop solutions corrodes the quality of work processes. Managers also worry about the loss of their own status and power in sanctioning employee involvement and growth. Much of management education has generally emphasized "control over the enterprise" and to "be on top of things." Sharing power, authority, responsibility, and decisionmaking is uncharted territory for some organizational authorities (Applebaum and Batt, 1994).

"Knowledge is power" is a popular idea. The truth is that knowledge is power when power lets it be that way. Power decides knowledge, not the other way around. Simply knowing something is no entitlement to use it. Change agents interested in encouraging learning have to confront the realities of power in organizations. Power in the age of mass production and the ascendancy of ideal-type bureaucratic institutions stripped workers of using their knowledge on the job. When the focus of knowledge changes in organizations, so does the locus of power. OD and a cluster of recent management reforms aim to restore employee know-how to its legitimate place on the job.

Hijacking What People
Know — The Seeds of Disempowerment

Organizational Development encourages the partnership of learning and change. Most modern management reforms are not self-consciously OD, but they share the intention of giving power to employees to participate in decisions. The movement toward creating conditions for learning and improving the quality of human capital is paramount in high-performing organizations. These goals are significant because they reverse an enduring trend begun roughly a hundred years ago that disrespected employee intelligence.

At the beginning of the twentieth century, organizations competed on a mass production basis that involved manufacturing high volumes of standardized goods and services at the lowest possible price. Mass production systems were responsive to the requirements of America's early industrialization period. In the public sector, a similar objective was to ensure that all Americans had access to mass-produced services such as education, health care, and law enforcement. Mass production methods were successful in providing Americans with a standard of living and quality of life unmatched in the world.

The unparalleled success of mass production methods in turn-of-the-century America is appropriately credited to the contribution of Frederick Taylor's (1911) idea of scientific management: the classic set of techniques to rationalize work. In the age of quantity mass production, the organization moves down the learning curve; knowing how to be ever more efficient in squeezing out variances that increase costs.

Scientific management is fueled by the bias of objectivism that work can be reduced to a blueprint, engineered, and totally controlled based on scientific knowledge. Taylor's methods bring all aspects of work under strict control. Taylor did pay almost complete attention to working knowledge, although in his negative view of it he tried to transcend it by turning experiential know-how into objective intelligence. Taylor intended to break the grasp of worker control of the knowledge of their jobs and passing that ownership to managers who would "assume the burden of gathering together all of the traditional knowledge which in the past has been possessed by the workmen and then classifying, tabulating, and reducing this knowledge to rules, laws, and formulae . . . " (Taylor, 1911, p. 36).

The reason managers had to take control of the knowledge system was to eliminate *soldiering.* According to Taylor (1911, pp. 32–33):

> The greatest part of systematic soldiering . . . is done by the men with the deliberate object of keeping their employers ignorant of how fast work can be done. So universal is soldiering for this purpose, that hardly a competent workman can be found in a large establishment . . . who does not devote a considerable part of his time to studying just how slowly he can work and still convince this employer that he is going at a good pace.

Because of the deleterious effects soldiering had on the productivity of the firm, it had to be stamped out. The employee knowledge system had to be commandeered and returned to the shop floor in the form of detailed rules, regulations, and standard operating procedures. From an OD perspective, what is represented in desire to get control of the working moves of employees is a set of mistrustful assumptions about people ands their attitude toward work (e.g., McGregor 1960; D. G. Carnevale, 1995). Organizational Development values are clear on the subject of people and whether they are trustworthy at work. Achievement, growth, development, and the search for meaning in life are natural human drives. People recognize the opportunity to realize these states of being at work, if they are permitted to do so. For example, recently I met family members at the airport and cleared security. Picking up my personal property, I heard a conversation between a supervisor and a new employee about the security job. The supervisor was letting his subordinate know what he considered important to check and what he could let go. The important point, he emphasized, "is to remember that it is a law of nature that people will do as little as they can get away with" and you have to behave accordingly as a supervisor. The legacy of Frederick Taylor endures.

Scientific management caused employees to lose control over the full expression of their work. The philosophy separated work into two parts—conception and execution. Through the use of intrusive analytic techniques like time and motion studies, the mental aspects of work was separated from its physical manifestations. Where once staff enjoyed a broad scope of action over their jobs, they were now deskilled, reduced to carrying out the directives of higher-ups. The consequences proved to be severe for front-line workers. As Braverman observes, "hand and brain become not just separated, but divided and hostile, and the human unity of hand and brain turns into its opposite, something less than human" (1974, p. 125). This state of affairs—hijacking employee control over the power of their own knowledge—is what OD has attempted to rectify ever since.

Learning

The value of what people know is now prized in organizations. It is recognized that participatory work cultures foster learning and authoritarian structures inhibit gaining knowledge. What people need is room to think and act, where conception and execution of tasks is reintegrated.

Learning occurs when people engage the work and respond to material. The resources can be another person in the case of a public employee service worker or it can be the felt sense that a group experiences when an idea on how an action might solve a problem in the corrections agency. Learning is the ability to process what is really happening and make adjustments based on judgment about what is going on and what is called for. According to Argyris:

> Learning occurs when we detect and correct error. Error is any mismatch between what we intend an action to produce and what actually happens when we implement that action. It is a mismatch between intentions and results. Learning also occurs when we produce a match between intentions and results for the first time. (1993, p. 3)

Learning can be superficial or it can be deep. Single-loop learning is of the simple variety. People have theories of action. When a person engages the world, there is an intention of a match between intention and outcome. If what is expected occurs, the agent is satisfied. If a mismatch occurs, the response to the error in action is to go to the same set of variables and manipulate them with identical intentions. This is single-loop learning. There is a change in action but not in the factors that are used to realize the intentions of the agent. Single-loop learning is also known as Model I learning and it is important to realize that it is not inherently bad or ineffective, especially in routine or programmed situations. It has its place in organizations.

A different way to behave when objectives are not realized is to change the governing variables. The idea is to go deeper or to think outside the controlling paradigm or operating frame. The importance of single- and double-loop dichotomies is that problems in double-loop thinking impair leaning. Learning often requires deviation from a set norm. The entire discussion in the previous chapter about resistance to change is about unwillingness to learn and to engage in double-loop thoughts. Double-loop learning is also understood as Model II and is most appropriate in nonprogrammed, nonroutine situations that are more and more common in the turbulent environments of organizations (Arygris, Putnam, and Smith, 1985; Argyris, 1982, 1993).

The result of learning is a change in behavior, assuming the learning experience is processed and internalized. Individual characteristics that encourage learning are:

- Abilities and skills concerning learning, that is, knowing how to learn.
- Perceptions, paradigms, frames, and willingness to change structural biases and be open to other ways of thinking about reality.
- Competence in reflecting upon experience, trusting it, and having the courage to change how to do things, given feedback about practice.
- Self-image or feelings of self-efficacy, agency, internal locus of control or belief that people can influence their lives.
- The courage to overcome internal resistance to change or the ability to overcome the fear that fresh knowledge often engenders as one's hold on life is challenged.

The individual is only part of the learning story. Individuals work in systems. How those systems are structured and maintained may encourage or discourage learning. For instance, it is not enough to send some staff to a weekend retreat to learn one thing or another and then return them to a work culture that systematically extinguishes what has been experienced. It is too common that the only way organizations measure what has been practiced is the classic "end-of-session smile barometer" where people rate what they have gained that day or couple of days. They are invariably positive. Weeks later there is no follow-up about the extent to which the learning was sustained or even used. In a moment of frustration, a colleague once remarked that our training efforts were only changing people's language, rhetoric, or espoused theory and not their behaviors. After a while, their organizations wiped out even that.

These experiences are not OD. They do not always bring people from the same organization together for learning. The process is customarily known as "training," comes from the outside, and is not the product of people interacting, sharing information, and learning together on real organizational problems. There are precious few action components where people try out what they have learned and report back to the group(s) for another iteration of group problem solving if initial strategies need adjustment.

Organizational factors that support learning include:

- Job design that gives employees room to make judgments about what the situation calls for.
- Organizational structure that is not so complex that unnecessary levels of review stifle initiative.
- Policies and procedures that are not rigid and zealously enforced.
- The use of work teams that permits employees to share information and be creative.
- Rewards and incentive structures that promote learning opportunities and knowledge acquisition.
- Leadership that supports risk taking in practice rather than theory.
- Assessing what people are learning and how that influences their work behaviors.
- Testing whether learning is continuous and sustainable.
- Respecting employee know-how.

It takes two things to make learning work in organizations. The first is an individual worker's ability to take responsible action, be open to feedback, suspend assumptions that blind feedback, trust working experiences, and make decisions based on what feels right in the particular situation. The second is creating an organizational culture that supports learning down the line. Human resources practices reward skill acquisition, prompt teamwork, enlarge the zone of action so that individuals can make judgments about what is best in a work setting, and treat employee knowledge with respect. Evaluations are made on the quality of practice that learning produces.

Liberating Employee Know-How

What does it mean to treat employee knowledge with respect? What is it like when a manager respects employee judgment? What does it mean when a manager puts aside position authority and relies on a subordinate for the welfare of a unit? The answer is found in an exchange from a popular movie, *The Hunt for Red October.*

In *The Hunt for Red October,* a conversation occurs between the character Jonesy, a sonar man, and the captain of an American submarine. The story line is that the Russians, the Cold War enemies of United States, had managed to accomplish something that would give them enormous tactical advantage in submarine warfare: They had produced a submarine that could run on a different kind of physics. The new technology could render a submarine's "signature," the sound it made when underway, baffling to American listening devices. The Soviet craft's new signature would not sound like a submarine or any other type of boat; it would be an elusive "waffle"; something somewhere between the sound of a whale and an undersea earthquake.

Jonesy is not an officer and has no power to command or take over a situation. He is, however, an experienced sonar man, very good at what he does, perhaps the best in the submarine navy. He knows what submarines sound like—or should sound like.

As the Soviet submarine engages its new drive to mask its location and breaks undetected into the open sea, the crew aboard the American submarine, waiting to track any Russian submarine that tries to break for the open sea, is stunned by the sudden "disappearance" of a vessel with the distinctive signature of a large Russian submarine. Where it went and how to follow it instantly became a puzzle of enormous proportions; one that the highly technical capacity of the U.S. vessel was not prepared to handle.

The captain of the American ship has all of the traditional power and authority that befits his status as the commander of a military vessel. He bears the ultimate responsibility for his boat and all hands stand by, waiting for him to issue orders about what to do. The captain has a model or paradigm about how Soviet submarines should behave and what they should sound like. He has a computer to help him deal with a number of contingencies that arise in any tactical situation. The computer features a memory track of every kind of underwater sound imaginable; even the sounds of whales and earthquakes. The problem is that the waffle of the Soviet vessel is like, but not exactly like, these things. To isolate its unique character, so it can be tracked, requires the kind of "ear" that only an experienced sonar man musters.

The captain sets aside his position of power, his superior authority, and lets go temporarily of what his idealized models say about Soviet submarines. He begins to talk with Jonesy about what is really going on. He defers to the hands-on experience of the person actually doing the listening to solve what is essentially a listening problem. He does not force his idea of what reality should be to decide the situation. Correspondence theories of truth are of little help here. He does not persuade Jonsey to hear something that does not really exist just to validate his idealized model. He does not use power to dominate for actual working experience.

Carefully, even artfully, Jonesy and the captain talk through the working experience, translating and retranslating each other's different ways of knowing in order to broach their separate sensory and conceptual worlds. Finally, they are able to agree on a sound they will track as the Soviet submarine. Reality later proves they get it right. The captain then resumes control of things; always, however, deferring when appropriate to Jonesy's "ear."

The story underscores the point that staff has an "ear" for the specialized nature of their work. Every employee lives in a distinct sensory world. Each worker knows something and is continuously learning more about the work and the organization. In the traditional model, managers do not trust exploring what know-how exists around them or have confidence that the experiential knowledge of staff adds to the knowledge base of the organization. Their idealized images of the world leave little room for contrary ways of doing things. These biases crush individual, group, and organizational capacity. Realizing learning in organizations requires mutually respectful dialogue where the merit of ideas is determinant, not power.

A second example of teamwork, learning, and dialogue in organizations is reflected in the movie *Apollo 13*. It is a story about a flight control center on the planet Earth staffed with every conceivable kind of scientific expertise and all of the computer and machine technology imaginable to control manned flights into space. When a member of a flight crew just having lifted from the planet's surface announces,

"Houston, we have a problem," a knowledge dynamic similar to the one evident in the film *The Hunt for Red October* begins to unfold.

For the remainder of the movie about this real historical event, a dialogue occurs between people on the ground, hierarchically organized, supported by everything science and pure reason can offer, and the flight crew, also backed by the same science. The flight crew, however, have their physical senses involved with the actual problem in a way that the ground crew can only imagine. Ground control is grounded, out of touch, in a very significant way, with the reality of the situation that is true to the flight crew. Ground personnel cannot experience directly what is going on in the space capsule although they can observe the survival problems of the crew through their gauges and computer output.

The successful rescue of the crew depends on the ability of everyone involved to translate between different—and relevant—ways of knowing about the problem. Dialogue—or meaningfully real conversation—is needed; one in which there is mutual respect between what the crew in the sky knows and what the ground personnel understand. Cooperation, not power, is called for. Power does not decide knowledge in this case. Organizational status is not confused with having the right feel for the truth of the situation.

The principals talk and listen, but most important, they trust one another's judgment. They try to place themselves in the situation of the other. One astronaut, for instance, grounded because of a threatening case of measles, climbs into a test capsule and works routines over and over again in the exact same way and under almost the same physical handicaps he imagines the actual flight crew is undergoing. He sacrifices sleep and tries, in every way possible, to re-create the reality his friends are experiencing. He puts himself into the workplace of the others.

Similarly, a ground crew uses the same materials available on the lunar module to assemble air scrubbers to reduce dangerous CO_2 levels that threaten the lives of the crew. Coming up with the solution to the problem begins with tossing assorted and seemingly unrelated materials onto a table and the charge is given to make something where a round peg item fits into a square hole. Power doesn't decide what happens next. The team works based on ideas and the ones that work become part of the solution. There is no manual for designing such an item and standard operating procedures are useless. It is a knowledge and learning problem. Creativity is necessary. Freed from their usual constraints, the team solves the problem based on constant exchanges of information, trials, learning, and eventually consensus.

Apollo 13 exemplifies teamwork, dialogue, the art of meshing different realities, working without advanced planning, and trusting the skills and competencies of people to do the right thing in a difficult situation. The case is underscored by high trust, the chance to exercise judgment, and respect among different people for the know-how of each other. In many ways, the movie represents the core values of OD at work. When students watch it, they immediately see much about shared leadership, group dynamics, organizational learning, authentic communication, and faith in the power of what people can accomplish when they work together in a fully collaborative fashion. The fact that the story is true makes it even more powerful. Many people have never experienced the same kind of pulling together for a common purpose where they work. For them, the learning or high-performing work organization is nothing more than an intellectual abstraction.

Action Research—The Core Problem-Solving Technology of OD

Action Research (AR) is the core technology of Organizational Development. There are many definitions of Action Research, but they all embrace common themes. For instance, French and Bell describe AR in the following way:

> Action research is the process of systematically collecting research data about an ongoing system relative to some objective, goal, or need of that system; feeding these data back into the system; taking actions by altering selected variables within the system based both on the data and on hypotheses; and evaluating the results of actions by collecting more data. (1999, p. 130)

The principal founder of Action Research was Kurt Lewin (1947 as cited in Bruce and Wyman, 1998, p. 13), who believed that the key

elements of Action Research were what he characterized as recon-
naissance, fact finding, changes in planning, and action based on a
correctional feedback system that linked action to facts.

Argyris (1993) develops a systematic approach to promote learning
and action based on learning. After dealing with roadblocks to learning, he concentrates on interviewing and observing the players in the
problem-solving situation, organizing findings for leaning and action,
conducting meaningful feedback sessions, dealing with trust, managing the clash between expectations and needs, and getting feedback
from below.

The essential thing about Action Research is its practical intent. The
process aims to solve a real problem. It is not part of a disinterested
search for knowledge. It is not pure research, it is applied. Action Research is a form of real world studies that unapologetically hopes to
intervene in a situation, learn about it, and change it through the participation of those with something at stake in the outcome. Action Research is a problem-solving change process (Robson, 1993). The apt
saying about Action Research is "There is no research without action,
and no action without research."

Action Research is not indifferent to learning from its processes.
Organizational Development and Action Research have their roots in
behavioral science methods (French and Bell, 1999). OD is data-based
and the unit of research is how well people perform in changing exist-
ing conditions and solving problems. There is a methodology and
rigor is demanded in interpreting behaviors and the meaning of
events. Action Research naturally focuses on case studies. These characteristics make action science a way of knowing through evaluating.
There is no one best epistemological and ontological set of research
methods. Action science promotes action with the human in mind.
Practical knowledge is its normative research ideal.

The Action Research process is a multistep, iterative process (see
Figure 4.1). It begins with the engagement of a change agent, usually
by executive-level personnel. The consultant change agent makes an
initial investigation and typically begins a process of joint action planning with the key client or client groups. Groups, for example, would
meet. There may be one or more groups in a room and the consultant

FIGURE 4.1   The Action Research Process

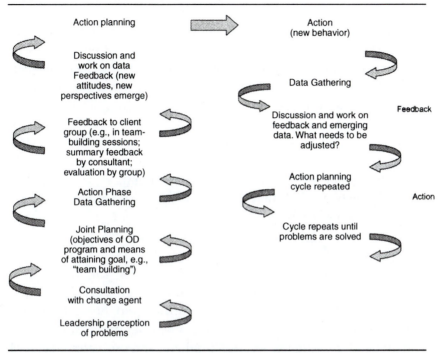

SOURCE: Adapted from *Organizational Development* by Burke, 1994, reprinted by permission of Pearson Education, Inc. Upper Saddle River, N.J. 07458

change agent would provide each group with the materials to support brainstorming about a problem. The consultant change agent would ask the group(s) a series of relevant questions, facilitate, data from the group(s) would be make public, usually by posting on the walls, and feedback is processed and reprocessed until some consensus is reached on what to do about the problem. The action or actions agreed to are tentative hypotheses or formulations about what to do to resolve the outstanding issue(s). The agreed action is tried, results are evaluated, and the feedback is used as the basis for the next cycle that repeats itself until the problem is solved. Participants learn by doing, by interacting with others, and by experiencing the outcomes arising from their theories of action. This method is the core that underlies all of the countless OD interventions available to a change agent. Action Research is generic OD and, although variations on the theme are common, the core process is the same.

Action Research embodies the core values of Organizational Development. *Democratic norms* are realized because AR encourages involvement, participation, and effective voice by staff. The underlying *humanism* of OD is represented because the AR processes foster human growth and development. *Optimism* is accomplished because there is faith that employees can solve their own problems, given the opportunity. Action Research is all about process, how things are done in organizations to solve problems. The involvement of clients in resolving their own problems teaches them important task and relationship behaviors. Action Research deepens commitment to solutions that clients construct.

Conclusion

A great deal of what is learned in organizations is based on the experiential know-how of what the rules do not say and the endlessly varied real work episodes that standard operating procedures cannot comprehend. Experience, feelings, intuition, and processing feedback are the elements of learning. Judgment always has its place too. Learning denotes freedom to evaluate what is called for in various situations. Learning requires space to act (Watkins and Marsick, 1993).

The requirements for individual, group, and organizational learning are antithetical to the powerlessness programmed in the mind-set of autocratic institutions where pervasive mistrust of employee know-how leaves no room for employee participation and development. The cliché that learning is power is betrayed by the real experiences of staff everywhere. Learning is power when power makes it so. There is a host of management reforms that come and go with regularity, but the bureaucratic work organization is still the dominant form in American society. The learning organization exists more in classrooms and weekend retreats than workplaces.

There is no change without learning. There is no movement beyond the status quo without the possibility of creative acts. Fresh futures are not the outcome of rigid ideas and the repression of people's development.

Note

1. Much of this introduction is taken from D. G. Carnevale, "A Synposium: The Human Capital Challenge in Government," *Review of Public Personnel Administration* 16, no. 3 (summer 1996): 5–13. Human capital is not normally addressed in the OD literature. There are normative ideals about involvement and participation and a good deal about how to get people to contribute and learn in organizational problem-solving situations. The point here is that much of OD, like most management reforms, including those of Frederick Taylor, are after worker knowledge and for good reason. Instinctively, people appreciate that it is valuable. What is suggested here is that the innate notion about the weight of employee intelligence has roots and is measurable. A basic orientation about human capital, its meaning and intellectual pedigree, is a necessary precursor to any discussion about Action Research and learning on the job.

5

Groups, Public Management Reform, and Organizational Development

A vast number of Organizational Development (OD) intrusions are explicitly tied to group dynamics. In some sense, almost everything OD concentrates on involves team building, broadly defined. The size and number of the groups may vary but bridging the interdependencies between people to create cultures of high performance is at the heart of teamwork. Group work in OD recognizes the importance of how individuals associate, identify, and affiliate with others at work. The group is at the heart of OD.

Groups and teams are not the same things, although OD is interested in both. A group is defined as two or more employees who interact with each other informally or formally within an organization. A team is identified as "interdependent individuals who share responsibility for specific outcomes for their organization" (Sundstrom and associates, 1999, p. 7). All teams are groups but not all groups are necessarily teams. There is a debate whether the terms "group" and "team" can be used interchangeably (e.g., Sundstrom, DeMeuse, and Furrell, 1990; Katzenbach and Smith, 1993). In this chapter, teams and groups are used in common. Each expression will mean:

1. There is more than one person collaborating.
2. The interaction is for official organizational purposes.
3. The group has a claim on organizational resources to perform its work.

4. The issue of cohesiveness is important to work-group effectiveness.
5. Task-related behaviors are important to work-group functioning.
6. Relationship or maintenance behaviors are crucial to team effectiveness.
7. Process issues are considered important to work-group accomplishment.
8. Groups may or may not be leaderless, self-directing, or facilitated in some fashion.
9. Work groups and teams have organizational objectives to realize.
10. The issue of learning is important to work-group or team success.

From an OD point of view, work groups and teams are part of the same continuum and typically exhibit similar behaviors. The idea is that work groups and teams are some number of staff formally organized and supported to labor on organizational problems. The keys to group success are the same. The pathologies that sometimes plague formal work groups of every type are identical as well. OD consultants create and use teams as a primary method of enhancing organizational change, learning, and performance. The work group is a powerful instrument that satisfies the affiliation or social needs of staff, creates a context for individual development, is a participatory instrument that encourages involvement and voice, and is a primary tool for establishing organizational learning. In these ways, group processes underscore basic OD values. The group has been an important focus of Organizational Development since the seminal Hawthorne Studies.

From Hawthorne on Up

Classical organizational theory was based on the emergence of industrial engineering, where jobs were highly specialized, rationalized, and individualized. The orthodox administrators did not recognize the potential of groups and had no idea of self-directed work teams.

Frederick W. Taylor's (1911) *The Principles of Scientific Management* represented shaping ideas of the classical approach. These concepts were later married to the bureaucratic theory described by Max Weber (in the Gerth and Mills 1946 translation). Weber provided a description of an ideal-type machinelike organization compatible with Taylor's engineering work principles. Both men believed management was in disarray. Favoritism, nepotism, a lack of consistency, and disorder was perceived as inefficient and a drag on productivity. These uneconomical factors could be rectified only by rationalism. Henri Fayol (1949) brought everything together. He boiled the rules of command and control down to four primary functions of management: *planning, organizing, leading*, and *controlling*. These activities constrained the individual, the principal component of the work process.

In general, traditionalists envisioned individuals as people untrustworthy to do good work without close supervision. Given this powerful assumption, it was seen better that staff perform jobs defined by their superiors rather than have much discretion in conceptualizing what should be done themselves. The idea of what was to be done was separated from how it was accomplished. Conception of work was estranged from how it was to be accomplished. Persons were evaluated and rewarded based on their personal performance, not on how they contributed to group efforts. That idea, evaluation of an individual independent of group contributions, is arguably the norm in work organizations even today. Groups were feared; they threatened control. They provided a counterforce to organizationally established norms. They did not fit into the structure of things, work processes based on long-linked technology or assembly-line ways of accomplishing tasks in factories and offices. Of course, the worst scenario was that groups posed greater propensity to unionize. Labor unions were a significant counterforce to the alienating effects of the industrial machine and, in the absence of laws to regulate labor-management relations, much violence spread throughout industrial America. Organizations saw unions as outside groups ready to upset the "happy family" illusion of the industrial machine.

Recognition of the importance of groups and teams began during the 1920s and 1930s with the classic Hawthorne experiments. These investigations were the genesis of the human relations movement, later the seed of Organizational Development as a field of study.

The focus of the experiments at the Hawthorne plant of the Western Electric Company concentrated on technical interventions, for instance, how varying degrees of lighting influenced performance. Over the years, several experiments were conducted and the researchers became increasingly aware that a key to production resided in how workers influenced one another's attitudes and behavior. The meaning of events was discovered important, not just the actions themselves. How things were done was consequential. Organizations were social systems where what workers produced and how they worked was a matter they controlled to a larger degree than traditionalists had imagined. There was discretion in all work that escaped even the most determined efforts at control (Bendix, 1963). Two of the researchers summed it up in the following way:

> The study of the bank wiremen showed that their behavior at work could not be understood without considering the informal organization of the group and the relation of this informal organization to the total social organization of the company. The work activities of the group, together with their satisfactions and dissatisfactions, had to be viewed as manifestations of a complex pattern of interrelations. (Roethlisberger et al., 1939, pp. 551–552)

A new concept was taking shape. There were social implications in the industrialization of work (Mayo, 1946), cooperation was as important as technological prowess (Barnard, 1938), and there was more to getting things done than giving orders (Parker, 1984). The classical approach was faced with an onslaught of thinking that confronted its command and control ideology. It was being disputed by the velocity of a fresh idea that not only opened the door to the importance of the meaning of work and individual commitment, identification, loyalty, and satisfaction, but especially the value of groups in organizations (Homans, 1950; Bion, 1961). What was known early in America's industrial history would not be fully embraced until the 1980s, when the country faced a serious challenge in competitiveness with other nations, part of a newly emergent world economy. The reform of management practice and the opening up to the ideas of teamwork and team building finally arrived.

The Instructive '80s—The Takeoff
Period for Management Reform

In the early 1980s, American industry went through a difficult economic downturn. Unlike other recessions, this one evidenced more fundamental and permanent structural problems in America's competitiveness, both at home and abroad. Quantity production, once the holy grail of public and private management, was replaced by a new set of competitive standards. The importance of groups had long been recognized in OD but the powerful downturn of the 1980s vaulted what was known about putting employees together into teams to enhance organizational performance into a more relevant and higher status. Competitive pressures intensified and became global. Quantity production and the low-trust, low-involvement human resources philosophy that supported it had to give way. The competitiveness problem in the private sector was in large part attributed to the fact that American management methods were no longer world class.

The problems facing the business sector paralleled those facing government at precisely the same time. Taxpayer revolts, for instance, that were manifest in the passage of Proposition 13 in California and Proposition 2½ in Massachusetts reflected a general negative mood about government taxes and services. The election of Ronald Reagan signaled that dramatic changes were coming. The revolution coming to government concerning management philosophy would sometimes be labeled differently than private initiatives but operated in the same way. Motivating staff, providing vision, responding to stakeholders of every type, emphasizing quality, and modifying the worst aspects of the bureaucratic model were the new universal values in administration.

The inventory of reforms is familiar. Perhaps the most notable for its acceptance as the initial turn in thinking were "excellence" programs spurred by the early work of Peters and Waterman, 1982. Japanese management programs became popular (Ouchi, 1981), especially the idea of "quality circles," which was the shaping idea for moving the interest OD had exhibited in groups into notice for the creation of formal teams. Total Quality Management (TQM) (e.g., Deming, 1986; Juran, 1988) then became the rage. Finally, "reengineering" (Hammer and Champy, 1993) materialized. The excellent organization transcended into the quality organization that subsequently evolved into the reinvented organization and, finally, the learning organization (Senge, 1990).

Government came late to the reform table but added two distinct creations for its own jurisdiction in the form of the National Performance Review (Gore, 1993) and reinvention (Osborne and Gaebler, 1992). These were pretty much variations on the themes that already existed elsewhere. Micklethwait and Wooldridge write:

> On the whole, cases of "best practice" springing out of the public sector are rare. In general all the public sector does is borrow ideas from the private sector. It often seems like a bureaucratic version of Chinese Whispers, with one group of people applying what they think another group of people have said. (1996, p. 324)

The criticisms of the public sector continued at the 1995 meeting of the Academy of Management when Henry Mintzberg argued that a skull and crossbones should be stamped on the cover of all new management theories with the warning "not to be taken by the public sector." Peter Drucker weighed in and said that remedies for operational improvement in government really came down to two things: endlessly patching up services or downsizing (Micklethwait and Wooldridge, 1996). Never a borrower be may be good advice but the fact is that the private sector spent a good deal of time, and still does, in looking for "best practices" to improve goods and services. A number of improvements are documented in government operations that may have influenced the ideas but they were made to fit the realities of the operational context of the public sector. Business does not own a corner on decent leadership, motivated employees, or concern for doing good work. Still, the bias that business is better endures and the public sector's efforts at administrative reform go unappreciated in many quarters. The truth is that much has been done and is being accomplished all of the time and one of the main tools is achieving better performance through teams.

The issue of management reform has spurred some debate among academics in the public administration community who voice thoughtful concerns about the implications of the term "customer" to describe the citizen's relationship with government. The label was perceived as fostering a distortion of the real standing of the citizen. The question is also raised whether the idea of expanding managerial discretion in the name of operational improvement was a violation of the basic ideas of governance. A fundamental concept in public administration is that administrators are duty-bound to carry out policy directives as scripted by legislative bodies. This point of view asserts that managers have no right to freewheel policy matters no matter that the motive was to better serve citizens. At bottom, the dueling perspectives are about the limits and legitimacy of administrative discretion.

The particular worry is that reinvention and reform in government administration violates democratic principles. If that is the case, then Organizational Development's insistence on worker voice and participation is part of the governance problem. OD supporters, in short, will argue that a democratic society need not wring its hands too much when its autocratic work organizations lose some ground to the will of its employees and citizens.

Vigoda and Golembiewski (2001) address the issue of citizenship and the so-called "New Public Management" (NPM). They support the fundamental ideals of the NPM, which is not surprising, especially given Golembiewski's contribution to public-sector OD. Still, they are critical of administration that is only partly committed to real citizen involvement in governance, a type of citizenship they characterize as "metacitizenship," where playing robust roles, not passive ones, are the real goals of people in mechanisms of governance. Citing Organ (1993), they encourage citizens to be more than passive customers or arm's-length antagonists to government. The message is an OD instruction writ large.

The issue of citizen rights to be truly involved in governance and to take advantage of such liberties is the same as the message of OD in the workplace. OD is a philosophy that demands that employees have rights concerning workplace governance. They have the obligation not to sit back and wait to be taken care of by higher-ups. They cannot sit on their hands and blame organizational authorities for not fixing whatever irritates their work lives. The message for citizens is the same. In the end, Vigoda and Golembiewski (2001) conclude that the New Public Management and a truly participatory citizenry can be reconciled and made workable in practice. The same idea is suggested by Riccucci (2001), who sees the tension between the opponents of the so-called New Public Management and its supporters as constructive for the field and the practice of public administration. Forcing people to choose between the duality of the New Public Management and some kind of ideal-type democracy is a false dilemma on its face.

Despite the New Public Management/citizen governance debate, public administrators have embraced the idea of reforming how government is operated. Administrators commonly embrace the host of programs detailed previously and do not worry much about the labels as opposed to practical results. Under pressure from several sources, change has become the order of the day. Models that promise quick relief are embraced. It is no doubt true that the promise of what particular reforms can do have been oversold in an almost evangelical way and employees at every level of government have become cynical about the "flavor of the month." Still, leaders search for something that will make organizations excel and employees, to their credit, embrace the newest reform model because down deep they value meaningful work and care about quality despite negative stereotyping. The OD assumption that most people want interesting and meaningful work holds true.

All of the reforms embrace common themes related to OD's democratic, humanistic, and optimistic values. Each, in its own way, is a theory of knowledge and learning. The truth is that organizations should treat people with respect. They must ask what employees think rather than give orders. Associations are encouraged to allow effective voice without reprisal. Learning cannot occur if information and ideas are not shared. The common mind-set and herd mentality are dangerous. Superficial learning is secondary to more advanced, critical thinking. Experiential know-how—realism—finds at least equal footing with idealism in the high-performance organization. Equally important, staff involvement and participation provide a competitive advantage. Finally, cutting-edge organizations administer reward and incentive plans based on group as well as individual achievement, or, at the very least, reinforce every behavior that advances creativity, no matter at what level of organizations they are spawned.

Despite the academic debate, citizens are not opposed to quality services and want their money's worth from government. If reforms increase access and involvement, then perhaps the all-too-common lack of trust in government will be reduced. The idea of creating more space for dialogue between the government and its citizens is consistent with fundamental democratic values. The trick is to expand administrative discretion without subverting the requirement of not fully mixing the role of policymaking and administration.[1]

All of the innovations since the early 1980s are similar. Every one tends to advance the following propositions.

Involving People Inside and Outside

A "customer" is defined to include people internal to the organization such as employees in other departments and those external to the organization such as taxpayers, contractors, regulators, and suppliers. The organization becomes "customer driven." Satisfying customers is perhaps the single most important goal in organizational reform, but this is not a radically new notion. Although customers were not central in scientific management, for example, their interests were hardly ignored—as long as satisfying them favored investment outcomes. Taylor, for instance, saw customers in ways familiar to contemporary quality enthusiasts when he observed:

> . . . the third part, the whole people,—the consumers, who buy the production of the first two and who ultimately pay both the wages of the workmen and the profits to that employer.
>
> The rights of the people are therefore greater than those of either employer or employee. And this third great party should be given its proper share of any gain. (Taylor, 1919, p. 136)

It is fair to say that this "third party," the people of contemporary society, are the source of everything in democratic governance and the perceived failure of bureaucratic institutions and elected officials to represent their interests is a primary source of the increasing lack of faith in government institutions.

A case concerning an unsafe road in the Southwest illustrates the collision between government ideas about idealism and the realism of citizens. People were concerned about the safety of a local road and were not satisfied that city officials were going to do anything about it. Not feeling that the city was fully responsive to their concerns, they called their own meeting to discuss the problem and invited city officials to attend. Over 600 citizens showed up at the church along with a handful of city representatives. The citizens had the government's attention. Citizens complained of more than 600 accidents on the road in three and a half years and wanted something done to improve its safety. Better law enforcement, slower speed limits, and structural changes were suggested. Then the bureaucrats took over.

The city engineer, armed with eighty slides, started by saying that the state does not count individual deaths in a wreck but only the number of cars where someone died. The engineer was interrupted by a woman who said, "I lost my daughter and grandson in a fiery crash on that road. They are not statistics, they were humans." Mercifully, a more senior engineer took the podium from the first engineer, who was complaining that he had ten slides left to show.

Later, the city council took the problem out of the hands of the bureaucrats and committed to a number of changes to improve road safety (Quigley, 2000). The point is that citizens serve the same function as customers and clients in business and not-for-profit agencies, but they have different standing in front of their government. Mobilized in sufficient numbers, they can force change and they can realize reform. It does not happen enough, but they can speak truth to power and their real experiences can trump the abstract idealism of the disengaged bureaucrat and politician. Trust is the winner when people who work in government and the people they serve listen to one another.

OD is all about establishing communication between the multiple interests that swirl around government, to get people in the same room, to facilitate ideas on how to solve seemingly intractable problems, and let the power of ideas, not power itself, dictate the right course of action. The road problem worked out in spite of the established system's belief that it knew what mattered and what should be done with people's concerns. Bringing eighty slides to a meeting to show people that the deaths they have experienced are not statistically significant exemplifies much of what is wrong with government organizations today. Too many officials refuse to listen to people. They see persons lower down in the hierarchy as technically unqualified to speak to matters of rule making and policy implementation. This is the triumph of scientific idealism over realism.

From an OD point of view, the knowledge biases of the organizational pyramid are difficult to overcome because of the subtle arrogance that the well-placed inside professional is inherently more knowledgeable than the ordinary employee or the typical citizen. The OD change agent can help change separatist attitudes between citizens and government officials. OD is a reliable tool to help administration, with its internal problems with staff and in using team building, to improve services. These activities increase the internal capacity of the public organization. What also matters is to connect the government with the citizens it serves, using essentially the same techniques. In both instances, it is important to understand the role of the OD change agent.

It is worth revisiting the appropriate role of OD change agent when dealing with teams in organizations. The change agent does not behave as a repository of technical expertise on the substantive work of the organization. The client group knows what to do and must be trusted to find its way through the process. The problem is to help the group discover what it already understands but cannot for various reasons process appropriately.

The change agent certainly represents command of a great deal of practical and theoretical know-how, but it is used to help other people determine ways to solve their own problems, much as a therapist counsels a client. A therapist does not declare, "This is what is wrong with you and this is what you should do about it." The patient gains insight about problems, looks at choices on how to resolve them, and then engages in action to try out and try on new ways of being. From feedback about those actions, the client makes necessary adjustments and keeps repeating the cycle until something workable is realized. The change agent's role is like that of the counselor; expertise is represented but it facilitates events rather than directs.

Facilitation in much of OD practice happens in groups. In the same community where citizens banded together to fix a road, future search conferences have been held on the quality of local education. Volunteers have come together to analyze the problem of wastewater treatment and the large group process has been facilitated and continuously televised so anyone in the community can see what is going on. I have worked with the city council as a group to encourage better group interaction, and that has extended to council-staff relations. These processes are known as Large Group Interaction Methods (LGIMs) and are predicted to spread throughout the public and non-profit sectors (Bryson and Anderson, 2000). Such activities complement the small group interventions that happen inside organizations but they are built on the same set of values and around almost identical process activities. The idea of getting everyone in the room to work on problems is increasingly well accepted and owes much to the tradition of OD.

Trust is enhanced when people know that they share values, are permitted participation, effective voice, and have rights concerning what is done and how things are accomplished. Organizational Development manifests all of these trust-related factors in its underlying assumptions and operating methods. It is common to see OD as a useful tool employed inside organizations to build community and group cohesion. It is equally positive as a way to reduce the alienation and cynicism that exists in the political system. That means supporting the case of public administrators asking citizens how they feel about problems and what they think ought to be done to correct them. The inside rationale for participation and voice has strong upside-outside potential as well.

The Virtues of Work Groups

Groups or teams have a number of qualities for individual and organizational effectiveness. Groups:

- Allow staff to work on projects with a degree of complexity beyond the range of individuals working alone.
- Bring a diverse number of talents, ideas, and experiences to bear on problems.
- Allow competing perspectives to be aired, which encourages functional rather than dysfunctional conflict.
- Promote employee training and learning.
- Recognize the realities of task interdependencies.
- Help employees develop greater self-awareness.
- Support employee needs for affiliation and acceptance.
- Afford employees more power and control over the conception and execution of their work. (Mohrman, Cohen, and Mohrman Jr., 1995; Yeatts and Hyten, 1998; Sundstrom and associates, 1999)

Of all the salutary effects of teams, many can be subsumed under the rubric of group learning. Groups are systems for learning. The diversity of experiences of a group interacts and produces synergy where the whole is more than the sum of its parts. Common OD training devices, for instance, used to underscore this important points are Lost on the Moon, Lost at Sea, and Lost in the Wilderness–type exercises where individuals are asked to imagine that they have suffered some disaster and have a handful of assorted items needed to assure their survival. Persons rank the items in order of importance and then join groups charged with the problem of producing a consensus list of the same material. Typically, the group solution to the problem is better than the average individual resolutions and it is not uncommon for the worst group to generate a better score than the best individual in the room.

The groups are "leaderless" since no person is put in charge. Team members organize themselves and perform the two classic roles necessary to be successful in any group situation—task and relationship behaviors. Success depends on paying attention to the problem to be solved and to the people charged with finding answers to it. The traditional OD belief is that putting people together to solve a problem produces better solutions than individuals alone can engineer. Just as important is the truth that people who labor together on an issue learn something about how to solve particular problems, but they also understand something about themselves and how they relate to other people. It is an invaluable catalyst for self-development. Although the exercises are simple and are not related to actual organizational problems, the core truth of the experience holds. People do more and learn more when they cooperate than when they try to go it alone.

The method most used by groups to generate options for problem solving is "brainstorming," where ideas are generated by members in a freewheeling fashion. The basic rules of brainstorming are: no criticism until all the ideas are out and then judgments on the merits can be made, imagination, mental leaps, and connections flow freely, people build on others' ideas, initially aim for quantity, and record each suggestion. Although brainstorming is the process, reaching consensus on an actionable initiative is the goal, that is, finding creative solutions that people trust will work and will try out.

Another popular group decision method employed by OD agents is the Nominal Group Technique (NGT). A group is brought together to discuss a problem. Individuals silently write down ideas or alternative courses of action that might resolve the issue. The ideas generated are recorded on a blackboard or flip chart. The thoughts are discussed and then the group silently votes for the concepts they think are most useful. The group is nominal because it has a reduced role in brainstorming—there is less talking about what is being proposed—and the mathematical outcome is different from a consensus solution.

Another group decision process is the Delphi technique. It is a procedure that generates ideas from a physically dispersed group, that is, not in the same room. It involves surveying experts repeatedly concerning a particular problem until the dimensions of the problem are specified and alternatives for action identified. For instance, the Florida legislature was interested a few years ago in whether it was state of the art concerning the problems of young people. A Delphi survey was conducted. It started by phoning experts known to the researchers as being involved with children's problems. At the end of each call, respondents were asked if they would participate in the survey. If so, they were then asked to recommend another authority in the area. Slowly and deliberately, a network or national panel of experts was identified. A questionnaire was developed and mailed, and the process began. Respondents were asked to identify the problems of children in America and to prioritize them. As surveys returned, they were analyzed and subsequent questionnaires were mailed. With each iteration the researchers were able to come closer to defining the problems and arriving at recommendations for resolution. The good feature of the Delphi is that it can bring a wide assortment of experts to bear on an issue when it is not possible to get them physically together.

The Delphi method is a process much like facilitating a group physically present in the same room. It involves asking people to define the problem, discovering common themes, ranking important items, and then taking the most important issues into group discussion about what actions might be taken to redress the problems specified. This is generic OD and runs through almost all of the group decision processes used by teams and groups of every variety.

There is much to argue in favor of organizing individuals into groups and encouraging teamwork. It is fair to say that turning to teamwork restored competitiveness to American organizations following the disastrous downturn in the 1980s. Effective use of group processes was one of the most important tactics that assisted American organizations to make the transition between the quantity paradigm to the quality model of production of goods and services.

Organizational Development must be credited for recognizing the importance of group dynamics as early as the Hawthorne Studies and committing to research how groups formed and functioned well before the latter part of the twentieth century. OD's appreciation of the importance of the human group was well before its time. Change agents pay considerable attention to group behaviors in organizations, especially when they are called on to help an organization work through assorted difficulties.

Downside Dangers of Groups

Groups have downside potential. There is so much enthusiasm about team potential, much of it well deserved, that the pathologies associated with groups are sometimes overlooked or undervalued. The problems with groups usually arise out of the phenomenon of cohesiveness and attendant pressures to conform to group norms.

Cohesiveness is the extent to which group members are identified with the group and its members. Cohesiveness is the extent of "being tight," sharing the same values, and being loyal to other group members and to the group as a whole. Cohesiveness is not inherently a negative force. Cohesiveness means there are more things pulling the group together than tearing it apart. Establishing a *reasonable* measure of cohesiveness is an appropriate and common goal of OD practitioners. If groups are successful, they need to be glued together in a real way. They also need to be well led.

A classic study that affirms both the positive and negative prospective of groups is the Schachter study (1951). In that research, it is found that cohesive groups have both positive and negative dynamics. The key to the kind of outcomes cohesive groups produce is directly related to how they are led. Researchers found that highly cohesive groups were a "time bomb" in the hands of management. Highly cohesive groups that were well led were extremely productive. Highly cohesive groups badly led were capable of restricting output. In other words, people who are tight do well when leadership is in good hands and are subversive and counterproductive when leadership is incompetent. The safest thing, of course, is to have low-cohesive groups. They are not dangerous but they have no potential for individual development, creativity, and high performance either, which are the primary objectives of the OD practitioner.

The question is, how much cohesiveness is enough? Cohesiveness is one of those things that statisticians term curvilinear. It is a good thing as it gets stronger and produces outcomes that are valuable. At some point, however, too much turns negative. For instance, a certain measure of anxiety is not all that bad for athletes and test takers in terms of performance in sporting events and in taking exams. At some point, however, when performance anxiety becomes too strong, both the athlete and the test taker can freeze up and be unable to perform at all. The same is true of cohesiveness. There is a point of diminishing returns with this construct. It is at the point where groups or teams are so rigid and overly identified that conformity reigns and critical thinking capacity evaporates.

Groupthink (Janis, 1982) is the classic dysfunction of excessive cohesiveness in a group. It is when members' striving for unanimity on issues overrides the ability to think analytically about their situation. When consultants urge groups of employees to "think outside the box," Groupthink is the box. Individuals refuse to deal with reality rather than appear as not being "on board," "with the program," or "team players."

The characteristics of Groupthink are:

- A sense of invulnerability, willingness to take risks, and a sense of being all-powerful.
- A sense of morality that leads to the belief that higher powers support the position of the group or that the group's perceptions are the unquestionably ethical. "If God had to choose a side, it would be ours" is the mentality.
- A tendency to rationalize away anything that disagrees with the group's worldview, that is, to deny data that should be investigated as consequential for the group's well-being.
- Self-censorship or driving out any evidence of dissent.
- Peer pressure employed to keep contrary ideas from being examined.
- The existence of mind guards or self-appointed mind police who are enforcers of the group's dominant mind-set. (Janis, 1982, pp. 174–175)

Another classic example of group dysfunction is the Abilene paradox (Harvey, 1988). The Abilene paradox evolves from a story of an extended family in Texas who are enjoying themselves playing dominoes and drinking lemonade on a hot afternoon. Someone suggests they drive fifty miles to Abilene for Sunday dinner. The car has no air-conditioning, the food is terrible, and people return resentful and unhappy. Finally, someone says they didn't want to go. Others pipe in that they didn't want to go either. As the truth emerges, no one wanted to go, but everyone was going along, being polite, not rocking the boat, and trying to be good family members as they thought they should. The real agreement was not to go to Abilene. There was public agreement to go and unanimous private agreement not to go. The group couldn't manage its real agreement not to go. Harvey's point is that organizations take trips to Abilene all the time. The question is, why?

The answer to why people don't speak their minds in the Abilene story is the same as it is in the Groupthink example. Staff fear that the truth will get them in trouble. This dynamic is found in the classic staff meeting when everything appears as if it is going wonderfully well on the surface. When a break occurs people go to the rest rooms or to the water cooler or coffee area and say, "If she does that one more time, I am going to let her have it," "Did you see so and so sucking up as usual?" "Why do we have these stupid meetings anyway?" "Those folks from personnel don't get it and never will." Then the meeting reconvenes and everything appears fine again. The trust is under the table. The truth is under the table. A friend once told me that when we were in such meetings, we ought to move passage of the hidden agenda and get things moving in the right direction.

As Argyris (1993) observes, the group is overprotecting itself, absorbed in organizational defensive routines, fearing embarrassment and rejection. Team members are inhibiting everyone's learning, including their own. The group is blocked and reality is hidden from view. In some organizations, this is understandable. If organizational authorities humiliate or shame people who come up with ideas contrary to the prevailing wisdom, those watching learn to keep quiet. If a person who speaks her mind in meetings gains a reputation as a troublemaker and is shunned by key officials, she learns to be quiet. Employees are always scanning their environments to learn what behaviors are acceptable and what are not. Leaders of organizations create the kind of quality staff input they deserve.

Group pressure can be powerful. The highly motivated work group properly balanced on task and maintenance behaviors, well led, with an ongoing commitment to processing new ideas, and with a commitment to learning can do much for the instrumental objectives of the organization and the self-development of its members. The highly motivated group, excessively cohesive, worried more about itself than what exists outside, obsessed with loyalty, critical of ideas that challenge its worldview, and punitive to nonconformists are a prescription for trouble in every way. Groups or teams are wonderful tools for making organizations and people better. They are not silver bullets and they do not operate on the right key without good leadership and support. There is nothing at all to suggest that teams cannot work in government and there is no respectable rationale that supports the notion that giving reasonable discretion to public administrators is a threat to the body politic. OD is a major tool to facilitate team building. OD's pedigree on group dynamics is unassailable.

Note

1. A truth not fully examined in the writings about the need to restore citizen trust in government is the reality that the politicians, who the traditionalists believe must set the public policy agenda, may not trust the people, which is why we get so much superficial talk from representatives of both political parties—safe talk—on message—careful in its yearning not to offend. The trust problem "in government" involves citizen perceptions that "government" is not trustworthy in its executive and legislative aspects (one might argue that the Supreme Court has unhappily joined the group after the most recent presidential election). To assume that the "lack of trust in government" is confined to the executive branch alone is questionable and that it runs one way. The government in all its branches may not trust the people.

6

Conflict and OD

Organizational Development (OD) is fundamentally about changing the dynamics of social systems. It is inevitable and natural that conflict is constantly in play when individuals, groups, and the organization try to come to terms with change. Conflict "means perceived divergence of interest, or a belief that the parties' current aspirations cannot be achieved simultaneously" (Rubin, Pruitt, and Kim, 1994, p. 5). The reasons for defensive conduct and resistance to change were detailed earlier. These behaviors can be understood as triggers of conflict. Change agitates people and naturally produces discord. Change also exacerbates the conflict already embedded in organizations. Change invigorates the tensions that normally lie below the surface in all organizations.

Social systems are full of assorted personalities, motivations, perceptions, and attitudes. No organization is of a single mind. In a positive sense, this is the diversity advantage where varying points of view can foster synergy and creative progress. The same feelings may be employed to subvert all possibility of vigorous teamwork.

Because people have dissimilar values, mind-sets, objectives, and visions about what an organization should be doing (clashes over ends) and how organizations should process work (arguments about means), disagreements are not uncommon. There are always scarce resources that encourage endless rounds of positioning for advantage. Assorted opinions abound about what is right concerning how people should be paid, how they ought to be evaluated, who merits promotion, and what people or units are most deserving to get the first crack at training or the newest technology. Another springboard of discord is power relations and politics of every sort. Contests of will, ambition, and mistrust are customary on the job. Organizations are networks of interdependencies and these often break down and generate dissension. People disagree about much in organizational life.

Persons may prefer that it were otherwise, but one of the essential truths of organizational existence is that conflict is an enduring reality. The question is not whether there will be conflict in organizations, but what kind of conflict will prevail.

The issue of conflict always begs the question whether it is functional or dysfunctional. The organizational philosophy evident at the beginning of the twentieth century saw conflict as essentially negative, something that needed to be stamped out. Discordant human relations were a threat to the normative goals of the machine, efficiency and harmony. Managers who had people problems in their shops were encouraged to stamp them out before they deepened or spread throughout the plant. Conflict was a clear menace to productivity.

Conflict can be a hindrance to productivity. Disagreements can escalate, deepen, and spread. They can lead to destructive outcomes between people and the longer friction goes unattended the more likely negative behaviors will increase (see Figure 6.1). When people dispute, they tend to see issues in a one-sided way. One piece of wisdom is that all conflict is the result of one-sided thinking. People's feelings and emotions are always engaged by perceptions that one's needs are blocked by another and cannot be realized. Typically, conflict escalates if it is not functionally addressed. It is all too typical that a cutting remark, a perceived slight, or disappointing treatment can soar into rage and then to violence in a matter of seconds. This is why organizations take conflict so seriously.

Unresolved prior conflict, problems that might not have been fully resolved or addressed at all in the past, surface when people contest. People search their memories for examples of mistreatment and use these instances to justify their present feelings of victimization. Mediators call this practice "sin-bagging."

Conflict spreads as the parties seek allies. Winning becomes important and the idea of making concessions is seen as losing face. These are powerful and natural feelings in humans. That is what

FIGURE 6.1   Spiral of Destructive Conflict

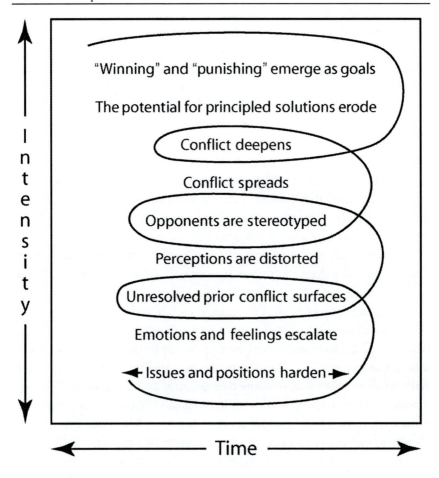

makes conflict so difficult to handle in healthy ways. Finally, communication between disputants becomes formalized, limited, or ceases altogether. The bottom line is that unresolved conflict disrupts necessary cooperation at work. Escalating quarrels displace attention to the work. People are bruised and commitment declines. Conflict ignored, unresolved, or mishandled is corrosive.

There is an upside to conflict. A disagreement has functional potential. It can clear the air. It can get how people feel out in the open. It encourages the interaction of ideas and the spread of information. In the open, differences can foster trust. However, there is much public agreement and private disagreement in organizations (Harvey, 1988). People wear masks at work and are careful how they express their true feelings. This behavior is rational in a number of workplaces where speaking truth to power is not welcome. People want to be accepted, to get along with the group, and fear embarrassment and humiliation. They refuse to discuss the undiscussable (Argyris, 1993). It is fair to say that a primary goal of OD is to break the silence, get under the surface of things, and open people and organizations to the truth of their situation. Differences are all right between people and work units. Working through them in a mature, beneficial fashion is always possible if people want to stop the various sorts of inauthenticity that are common in workplaces.

Although third-party peacemaking is a conventional OD tool, it has not received the direct attention it warrants. The use of grid OD and team-building exercises traditionally receive considerable attention. Growing notice is provided for future search and Large Group Interaction Methods. Still, conflict lurks at the heart of each of these techniques and dispute resolution work is an important process of facilitating transformation. There is no team building that does not deal with conflict resolution to some degree. Any gathering of multiple interests requires some attention to ironing out differences. Dispute resolution is an independent tool in OD used to tackle situations that are clearly about people in severe disagreement. Moreover, conflict resolution, like communication improvement, is always involved in OD interventions. Third-party peacemaking is a core OD competency.

An example of the role of conflict resolution in a case of Organizational Development arises out of a consultant contract to help a city that has serious problems with three of its unions in achieving labor agreements. Upon investigation, the problem is more than just a bargaining table issue that would suggest a direct peacekeeping approach with the unions and management over whatever issues were outstanding between the parties.

In this case, questions arise whether some of the negative things that the unions say at the table about the job satisfaction and morale of all city workers are true. It is problematic to try to access the sentiments of everyone employed by the city without committing an unfair labor practice by going behind the union.

Tensions that appear embedded in other relationships in the community have led to greater reliance on Large Group Interaction Methods, where citizens are invited in to participate in policy determination. This is a good idea, but even progressive action is not conflict free. Minority reports of group work are not uncommon. Permitting people to participate and be involved does not ensure happy outcomes (Luke, 1998).

In this case, dealing with the disagreements is not just a union-management difficulty, nor is it something that can be fixed through survey research with the employees at large, nor is it resolved by inviting citizens to study issues independent of the internal issues faced by the city. There are, in short, inside and outside problems and a single intervention technique is not suitable to help the parties address their problems. One thing is true: No matter what methods, hybrid methods, or multimethods might be used, dealing with conflict is necessary throughout.

At bottom, the city is in a conflict fix. Like most systemic problems, the surface dilemmas are surrogates for win-lose motivations and competing values. Ingrained discord about how the city should operate is apparent. A blaming culture is evident and strong emotions typically abound. Confronting the apparent tribulations means getting to the fundamental disputes that underpin and drive the difficulties. As this example instructs, conflict is at the heart of the matter in OD problem solving.

Third-Party Peacemaking

Third-party peacemaking is the term for the kind of intervention used in OD to help organizations process conflict. It is based on a human relations model of peacemaking where the psychological states of persons at the work site become the focus of attention. The basic model relies on two things: getting people to say what they think in an assertive way and listening actively to what others have to articulate about their feelings. It is a communications model.

People in conflict are much better at expressing what they want and what they need than they are at really hearing what other parties are expressing. The OD change agent performs a mediation function in dealing with organizational conflict. The OD practitioner works to ensure that what is relevant is expressed and what must be heard is honored. The idea is to facilitate, not direct, the parties toward real exchange of attitudes. The ultimate goal is to work with the parties to find solutions that both can honor.

In nearly all OD interventions, facilitating negotiations among parties is always part of the intervention agenda. Conflicts may involve interpersonal, interorganizational, and intraorganizational disputes.

Speaking Out Assertively

The first step in the peacemaking process is to get individuals to speak out authentically (see Figure 6.2). This means, first of all, that persons express themselves assertively, which means to exhibit behaviors that satisfy one's own needs and concerns (Zuker, 1983). Assertive speech is not passive or avoidant nor is it aggressive or forcing and attacking to get what one wants. Human aggression is a special problem in human relations and can lead to more than strong talk. It is a precursor to violence (Geen and Donnerstein, 1998; Allcorn, 1994). Assertiveness reflects a healthy level of self-esteem or a person's sense of self-worth. It is also a reflection of agency or the belief that one's behavior can make a difference. Assertiveness gives a feeling of power; it is a psychological state of self-efficacy, which is a person's belief that they can successfully achieve something (Bandura, 1995). Internal locus of control is a related concept (Rotter, 1975). It means that a person believes they control events in their lives, at least to some degree. They do not think of themselves as helpless in the face of external forces.

The assertive side of the dual concern equation of self-assertion and active listening is about the self or "I" (Buber, 1958). It is what I want and what I need. In conflict, most persons have little trouble working this side of the model. In sum, the psychological bottom line of the assertiveness vector is a healthy belief that a person's values and needs are worth hearing in an organization. There is nothing wrong with self-interest and healthy conflict management processes allow it to surface and be considered. It is a necessary step in resolving differences.

FIGURE 6.2 Assertiveness and Active Listening

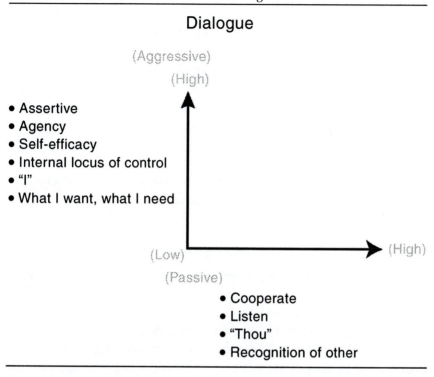

Dialogue

(Aggressive)

(High)

- Assertive
- Agency
- Self-efficacy
- Internal locus of control
- "I"
- What I want, what I need

(Low)   (High)

(Passive)

- Cooperate
- Listen
- "Thou"
- Recognition of other

The Problem of Listening

People speak about what they want better than they listen to what others want, at least early in facilitated negotiations. When parties confront one another at the beginning of negotiations, frustrations, anger, and expectations that needs cannot be met because of the other person can surface at that point. One-sided thinking is typical and persons become positional, that is, they have a single idea of what a good outcome ought to be: their own. Feelings of anger are common and distorted perceptions are usual. Selective listening, or hearing what one wants to hear, is characteristic.

Active listening is a form of cooperation or collaboration (see Figure 6.2). It is recognition of the Thou (Buber, 1958) or the worth of the other person as an entity independent of one's own needs. In listening to the other—really listening—one confirms the other's worth or being. Listening in real terms legitimizes the other and encourages a person to take seriously the story of the other. Actively listening demonstrates a willingness to see one's position as a series of assumptions that may or may not be "true" without the intersubjective agreement of the other. Finally, active listening involves trying to comprehend what the other person feels is important and why their way of thinking is so meaningful. Rephrasing what others are saying shows that listening is really going on. People will not listen unless they are sure they are being listened to. Attention is paid both to the substance of the matter and its emotional content of the speech of the other. It is possible to listen without hearing. Active listening is hearing the person and his or her ideas, feelings, and needs.

Dialogue

Dialogue is an unfolding process where parties freely interact and learn from one another. This aspect of dialogue results in conflict becoming functional, a catalyst for creativity, a joint interpretation of the world. Dialogue derives from two roots: "dia," denoting "through" and "logos," signifying "the word" or "the meaning of the word" (Bohm, Factor, and Garrett, 1991). Dialogue is a particular kind of communication, deeper than a conversation, more meaningful than discourse, and much more significant than the idea of simple discussion. Dialogue is not superficial back-and-forthness. Dialogue is real talk and is the integration of assertiveness and active listening.

Dialogue strikes at the heart of the pathologies of pseudo-speech. According to Bohm and Nichol, "the object of dialogue is not to analyze things, or to win an argument, or to exchange opinions. Rather, it is to suspend your opinions and to look at the opinions—to listen to everybody's opinions, to suspend them, and to see what all that means" (1996, p. 26). Dialogue arises from spatial interaction between participants—the room between persons where relationship is established. Dialogue confirms the other. It is a different kind of thinking. In dialogue, people suspend mind-sets that trap them into positional negotiations. The interaction between people is spontaneous; it is not based on rigid, positional beliefs. People can let go of cognitive and emotional baggage that attends the confrontation of hardened ideas.

Dialogue is an unfolding process of creative participation. It is the foundation for learning.*

Working the two vectors of assertiveness and active listening, the OD change agent creates conditions for dialogue and learning between individuals, groups, and within teams.

Working the Space—The Matter of Styles

All negotiations involve strategic choice. Figure 6.3 outlines the usual options that persons engaged in conflict face. Basically, the alternatives involve parties' concern for their own interests (assertiveness) and interest in satisfying others' outcomes (active listening). The model was originally developed as a way to understand differences in conflict style, which means it addresses the way a person normally deals with disputes (Blake and Mouton, 1964; Thomas and Kilmann, 1974; Ruble and Thomas, 1976; Rahim, 1983; Pruitt and Carnevale, 1993). The moves and their meaning are as follows:

- Competing is a style high in assertiveness and low in cooperativeness. It is a forcing approach commonly understood as win-lose or zero-sum. It asserts at a high level bordering on aggressiveness and listens little to the needs of the other side. Competing has its advantages. It is useful when quick action is required and protects persons from being exploited. It is the fight reaction to threat.
- Avoidance is unassertive and uncooperative. It is passive. It is flight. It presents the OD agent with the problem that one cannot be helped if they are unwilling to assert their claim and will not cooperate either. Getting this type of individual out of his or her protective shell is necessary if any resolution is achieved. Avoidance is as bad as aggressiveness. It is useful when the issues in dispute are nonconsequential to the person.

---

*The section on dialogue is borrowed heavily from work conducted by Gary Holmes of the University of Oklahoma concerning conflict, storytelling, and existential trust.

It is wise when more information or time to think about the problem is necessary. It is essential when faced with violence.

- An accommodating style is unassertive and highly cooperative. It is also known as appeasement or smoothing. The problem with this approach is that the person gives away to the other and doesn't assert their own needs. That might be wise when one wants to make a concession to demonstrate good faith or to get bargaining unstuck. However, if one continues to yield in the face, for instance, of a competitive person, the behavior is known as "feeding the tiger" and the competitive person may not reciprocate concessions, thinking the accommodator is weak.

- Compromising is a common conflict style. It is an intermediate move between assertiveness and cooperation. It is "horse trading" and makes sense when the issues are not deeply important to either side and is a good way to move negotiations along. However, it is not always the astute thing to do. It is sometimes believed that a compromise is fair because "both sides hate it." If that is the case then it is likely the bargain will not be honored. Finally, some issues are a matter of principle and are not divisible. There are a host of issues in public policy that sides will not compromise. Abortion, oil drilling in Alaska, stem cell research, capital punishment, and other topics are not easily brokered.

- Collaboration is the normative style on the board since it is high on assertiveness and collaboration, that is, people say what they want in a firm but not forcing way and listen actively to what the other side has to express. This is the win-win corner of the board and is also known as a principled, integrative, and problem-solving style.

As is the rule in all of public administration, "there is no one best way" to negotiate or to deal with conflict. Certainly, it would be ideal if all persons approaching disputes were collaborative, but that is simply not the case. The truth is that the OD practitioner has to be able to behave in every way on the style board and be capable of moving other persons along until they are in a reasonable, assertive,

FIGURE 6.3   The Interaction of Negotiation Styles with Interpersonal Dynamics

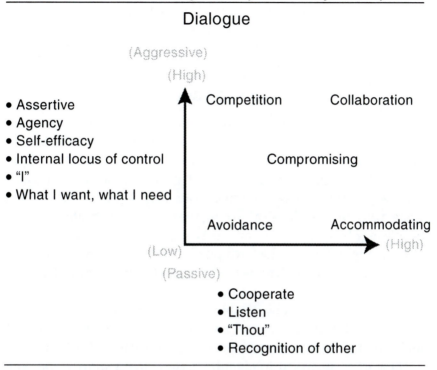

and active listening stance. A change agent may have to use every style in a single dispute case, often in the same hour. The OD agent needs to be able to recognize what styles are being used by the parties in a change situation and know how to deal with them. In the end, OD change agents have to be seen in conflict situations, as they are in all interventions, as honest brokers, interested in helping the parties solve problems. OD change agents are always the guardians of the process of dialogue.

Dialogue can be reached in many ways. "Interest based" is the most contemporary and the one promoted in government agencies, especially federal institutions. Interest-Based Bargaining (IBB) mimics closely the group process intervention methods of traditional Organizational Development. It creates leaderless groups, uses brainstorming as the principal problem-solving technique, and seeks consensus on what actions to take to solve problems. It is a group action research model facilitated by change agents. It is how "win-win" works in practice. IBB is "a joint problem-solving process conducted in a principled way that creates effective solutions while improving the relationship" (National Mediation Board, 1997, p. 7).

Interest-Based Bargaining

Interest-Based Bargaining (IBB) is generic OD. For instance, there is a decided team-building aspect to the process when groups are involved. The facilitator chooses to concentrate on the discord underneath or the manifest surrogate issues that are espoused as the reasons for low group performance. Either way, what is essentially bothersome will surface. Physical arrangements can be theater style or people may be seated at several separate tables, depending on the size of the group. If there are just two people, they can sit side by side facing the facilitator in traditional mediation style. There are just three basic objectives at the outset that are typically OD. First, get the relevant people in the room. Second, establish seating arrangements that do not encourage adversarial relations. Third, everyone's attention is directed to the front of the room for guidance from the faciliator/OD agent.

The parties are asked to identify "issues" that require resolution. An issue is a subject under discussion or in contention. Issues are the problems to be solved. The parties are not asked to give their position on these matters because positions don't identify problems. Positions provide one side's idea on how to solve a problem. They encourage people to insist on their own point of view, to act in their own self-interest. It is common for people in dispute to have different notions of the character of the disagreement. Getting at the problems, not the positions of the parties, is the necessary first step in achieving integrative solutions to disagreements.

The next step asks people why the issue is a difficulty. This is the process of uncovering the interest behind the disagreement or what is required to solve the predicament. Interests are broad conceptions of the dispute. Opposed to positional, or dealing with one party's proposed solution to problems, interests open the door to brainstorming, consensus, and creating more than one or two thoughts to solve dilemmas.

Group members are given flip charts or hardboard cards to write on. The process works the same as it does, for example, in group training, strategic planning, visioning, or team-building exercises. Probing questions are posed. The individuals or groups brainstorm until they reach consensus. The ideas are placed on the writing materials and posted for everyone to see. The ideas are the beginning of the "invention of ideas for mutual gain." The goal is to help satisfy the other party's interests as well as one's own.

The groups then identify standards or criteria to evaluate the written options. Generally, standards for determining solutions are based on the original interests of the parties. Options are evaluated against the criteria and those meeting the standards are adopted. If no alternatives are found that fully satisfy the criteria, those with the most promise are retained and recycled into the groups for further work.

IBB is a progressive and wise method of handling disputes. It complements the various group process models already employed in OD. It is participatory, provides staff with effective voice, and is optimistic that persons can work out problems. From a conflict resolution point of view, IBB combines assertiveness and collaboration. In the end, there is no peace unless people learn to assert their claims in a reasonable way and to listen to how other people feel about their interests. Much conflict is buried in organizations, creating tensions, resentments, and grudges. These feelings are corrosive. They destroy relationships. They subvert productivity. Ultimately, organizations that do not face differences in a healthy way reap anxiety and lower performance. IBB and the model of dialogue are answers to these dysfunctional consequences. They are strongly embedded in the peace-making traditions of OD.

Conclusion

There are a number of OD interventions. These can be combined into as many ideas for bringing people together for productive purposes as imagination can generate. Underneath much of what is wrong in organizations is the problem of conflict. It strikes at all levels of organizational analysis: individual, group, and organizational. It is interpersonal, intraorganizational, and interorganizational. Nearly every

OD intervention deals with some level of conflict as part of its method.

Conflict resolution is especially salient in public administration because public institutions are just that—public. They are nested in a vortex of competing stakeholder demands and charged with trying to carry out legislative mandates that are often unclear. Value consensus does not exist in American society, which means that fights about various public policy matters go on year after year. Often, the public administrator bears the brunt of these disagreements. The cause is not hopeless, as many public jurisdictions recognize. Getting parts of the community in the room and taking the time to work through policy issues has produced many successes. The OD values of democracy, humanism, and optimism are powerful antidotes to one-sided positional thinking that feeds discord.

The same is true in organizations. Conflict at every level can be worked out. Disputes can be functional. It is not the law of gravity at work that discord need be dysfunctional. Persons have a choice about what kind of conflict will exist. Methods are available to help administrators and most of them fall under the rubric of Alternative Dispute Resolution (ADR), which has been adopted in many governments to deal with disagreements. The ADR model presented here is in two forms. First is dialogue, or the combination of assertiveness and active listening. It is a communications model and incorporates how various negotiations styles fit the underlying dynamics of the ideal. The second model is Interest-Based Bargaining, fundamentally the same as the dialogue approach but presented much like what might be characterized as generic OD. In this case, groups are given the traditional working tools of the OD process, engage in brainstorming, post their ideas on charts, evaluate options for mutual gain, and then take action based on a set of agreed-upon criteria rather than rely on power to determine outcomes.

Conflict is ubiquitous. Administrators spend considerable time dealing with discord in their organizations. Managing conflict is a skill and it is an important area in Organizational Development. It warrants more direct attention than it has customarily received as an area of education, training, and development in the field of public administration.

7

Basic Values and Prospects

Organizational Development (OD) is more than a set of techniques. The myriad interventions used by OD practitioners are essentially facilitative; they are process oriented. However, these procedures are expressions of a deep array of humanistic values and assumptions. The core attitude of Organizational Development supports the participation and development of people in organizations. The heart of OD is realizing human potential at work. Organizational Development is optimistic about what people can achieve and decidedly depends on high trust. The spirit of OD is not the edifice of its operating methods but the foundation of principles that support them.

OD appreciates work arrangements as forms of governance and embraces a general democratic, bottom-up orientation. OD is not, however, indifferent to the instrumental goals of organizations. OD links productive issues with human ones. This connection acknowledges work institutions as social systems as well as industrious ones. OD sees productive outcomes directly related to human resources practices.

There is an enduring bias that supposes Organizational Development is "soft"—a program to make people feel good about their jobs rather than doing them well. This is the "touchy-feely" rap put on OD. The line is that there is too much relationship preoccupation in OD and too little consideration of task. The criticisms infer that a sterner or more diligent approach to management is the key to getting good work done. The hard school of organizational management concedes that there is no harm if workers feel good about what they do but it is not absolutely required for high performance.

OD is a philosophy about people and work, about the role of labor in the development of persons, organizations, and societies. OD cannot be categorized as either soft or hard. Thinking in these simplistic terms poses a false dilemma. Soft or hard are dualistic ideas and, like all dualities, untrue on their face. Counterpoising the extremes of a single continuum is a limited way of understanding the world.

The issue of what works in getting good work done is subtle, artistic, reflective, and embedded in nonlinear physics. It is not one thing or another, soft or hard. To conceive work methods as either hard or controlling misunderstands how work is accomplished in social systems. Thinking that the key to good work lies entirely in the human side of enterprise can be counterproductive and even manipulative. OD cares about getting good work done and quality products and services delivered. OD simultaneously embraces the notion that developing the full potential of people is an asset in every kind of enterprise. Involving people meaningfully in solving productive problems is catalytic and an important element in creating conditions for high performance.

The Problem of Trust

Trust is "faith or confidence in the intentions and actions of a person or group to be ethical, fair, and non-threatening concerning the rights and interests of others in social exchange relationships" (Carnevale, 1995, p. 20). Trust is institutionalized in an organization's rules, roles, and relations (Fox, 1974). Trust is ubiquitous in organizations. Trust is recognized historically by several classicists in the field of organizational studies as an important issue in the study of work. Trust is associated with productivity (Golembiewski and McConkie, 1975), group performance (Zand, 1972), cooperation and conflict (Deutsch, 1973), leadership styles (Likert, 1967), managerial assumptions about employees (McGregor, 1960), need satisfaction (Maslow, 1954), Organizational Development (Golembiewski, 1986), communication (Mellinger, 1956), psychological contracts (Argyris, 1960), the quality of labor and management relations (Reich, 1987), and "administrative evil" (Menzel, 2001). This does not exhaust the full range of connections between trust and organizational practices but it should suffice to give the reader an appreciation of its importance in organizational life.

Fresh perspectives warn that trust at work remains a significant issue. Marsden looks at the problem of jobs being "low trust-low discretion," and hopefully indicates that "if one recognizes the element of choice, for both workers and firms, between different ways of organizing their economic transactions, then the regulation of work roles and the problem of workplace trust emerges in a different and complementary perspective" (2000, pp. 173–174). In other words, trust is choice. Cooperation is choice.

OD is implicitly and explicitly concerned about trust. One area of interest is how Organizational Development encourages human development on the job. There are essentially two models about human development at work; each is positive in its own way but one is stronger, more advanced than the other.

The first human development perspective allows staff more control over the conception and execution of their work. Implicit in this model is the idea that increasing control and discretion is developmental. This approach is popularly known as "empowerment" and is found, for instance, in teamwork initiatives.

Organizations can go beyond the implicit human growth that comes from greater self-efficacy and agency (empowerment) and invest directly in the human capital of the workforce. This is an investment strategy and contains a measure of risk (compare with Creed and Miles, 1996). The organization has to trust that the employee will not leave to go to a better-paying position, for example. In that case, the organization that provided the learning opportunities is a victim of its good citizenship. This is no small problem. As Applebaum and Batt (1994) note, increasing worker competence increases the portability of worker skills, making employees more attractive to competitive firms that do not have an investment in human capital strategy. These firms simply steal the investments of competitors by increasing wages in the labor market. Perhaps that is not bad if all firms had an investment strategy. Skills and wages would rise everywhere, but that is not the case. The investment strategy is more beneficial to staff than the empowerment approach but it is risky for organizations that make the skill-building investment. Public policy that rewards organizations that invest in human capital is what is needed. It would replace mistrust in investment approaches and build on what is accomplished in the employee empowerment model in terms of staff development.

Hierarchy

"Where you sit is where you stand" is an old aphorism. Organizations, for the most part, tend to be hierarchical. The OD practitioner needs to appreciate trust from the point of view of someone subordinate in the hierarchy; a mechanism for control with attendant power to reward, punish, assign work, set the agenda, and be the legitimate voice of authority. When change agents approach the subordinate workforce, it faces a full array of resistances and defensive conduct that I discussed previously. However, traditional resistances are compounded if there is a lack of trust of the change agent or the organization's higher authorities. The issue is not just fear of change but feelings about trust that form the social fabric of every organization. Towering hierarchies exacerbate problems of trust. Their bureaucratic tendencies are a "monument to distrust" (Carnevale, 1995).

Bureaucratic work arrangements ideally provide various levels of segmented work units led by neutral professionals who perform highly specialized work roles, respect upward authority arrangements, and take care that subordinates follow standardized rules and procedures (Weber, Henderson, and Parsons, 1947). The bureaucratic, mechanistic model is much criticized in public administration. Despite its obvious virtues at the turn of the century in helping America become an industrial power, its use in a high-tech global economy has come under serious question. It is seen as stifling and too inflexible to cope rapidly with changing circumstances. Bureaucratic reform has become important in government. Still, it remains the dominant structural arrangement in the United States in both the public and private sectors. Despite "flattening hierarchies" or "turning bureaucracies on their heads," the ideal-type bureaucracy is still prevalent. We have bureaucracy triumphant. Is that fatal to OD?

Leadership and Change

It all starts at the top. No OD intervention can succeed unless it enjoys the support of the leadership of the organization. The change agent might have the notion to create an organizational culture where everyone is a leader. That is fine, but getting the support of top leadership is a threshold problem in any cultural change design.

There are a lot of theories about leadership. Ideas about leadership are a growth industry. Students of public administration are exposed to several suppositions about leadership so there is no need to cover the same ground to a great extent here. However, there are some things that are worth noting about leadership, the enthusiastic rhetoric that seems to accompany recent approaches, and OD.

Leaders can influence change in organizations, even bureaucratic ones. There are multiple theories of leadership and no one approach is considered ideal (Yukl, 1994). Of the various methods, the one that is most compatible with the ideals of Organizational Development is Transformational Leadership.

Transformational Leadership (TL) is a process where "leaders and followers raise one another to higher levels of morality and motivation" (cited in Yukl, 1994, p. 350). Bass (1985) extends the definition of TL mostly in terms of how transforming leaders generate a number of positive feelings in followers. In contemporary terms, the transformational leader typically has a number of attributes that include vision, empowering attitude, good communication skills, trustworthiness, and charisma. More than anything, the transformational leader commits people to action, to change, to transforming how organizations work, and what they represent. The powerful relationship between the leader and the followers is transformed into action.

Organizational Development has a bias for the transformational leader because she or he is committed to create conditions for the high-performing work organization. Notions of Transformational Leadership massage all the right biases in OD. The ideal transformational leader represents the core values of OD: optimism about what employees can accomplish if given a chance, encouragement of democratic values like the right to participate and the entitlement to effective voice, and nurturing the ideals of humanism, a philosophy where the worth and development of the individual is honored.

Labor Relations

A fair criticism of the OD literature is that it neglects the fact that many public organizations are unionized. In fact, the extent of organization of public employees in the United States outstrips that found in the private sector. Much of what OD covers concerning interventions runs into the scope of traditional negotiations and requires bargaining or some form of labor-management cooperation to make change. There have been a number of labor-management partnerships on a wide variety of issues. Most deal with some sort of organizational change not covered by the labor agreement. The message to change agents should be clear. There is a third party in the workplace, the certified representative of employees, and it has a proper role in change. That fact needs recognition in the OD literature because it is a reality in practice. Public-sector change agents constantly confront this reality (see Kearney and Carnevale, 2001).

They Know the Answer

Change agents share a common experience. No matter the intervention, when employees are asked any question they tend to brainstorm a series of options for discussion and evaluation. Without fail, there are themes across groups when they are asked what is good about the organization, what needs to be improved, and to identify the single most important priority they would choose to improve operations. In every organization there is the truth. Organizations that ignore it operate in delusion, out of touch with reality. Organizational Development connects organizations with what people know and then helps to place staff knowledge into action. The truth of what is and the potential to creatively find answers to problems reside in every work group. Staff did not begin to have ideas in the 1980s when reform after reform was introduced in organizations. The reforms mainly restored what had been taken away at the turn of the century. OD has always championed involving employees at work. OD is not late on the empowerment scene and is not a fad. Trust the group.

Power and Politics

Lasswell's classic definition of politics is about "who gets what, when, and how." Like trust, politics is a factor in every interpersonal exchange in organizations. Politics permeates the work environment. Politics has been treated much like conflict. It is often seen as negative and dysfunctional, something that should be repressed or driven away. People complain constantly in organizations about the level of politics. Staff categorize politics as a form of game playing, inauthentic behavior, ambitious self-interest at the expense of others, and generally untrustworthy conduct. Politics is usually not talked about in positive terms.

Organizational politics involves intentional acts of influence to enhance or protect the self-interests of individuals or groups. Like conflict, there will be politics. The question is, what kind of politics will there be? There is nothing unfair or unusual that persons with different points of view, honest aspirations, deep commitments to certain organizational visions, and urge for change in the status quo will compete for organizational resources or try to imprint their ideas on the organization as a whole. Organizations can be marketplaces of ideas that compete ethically for attention.

It is ethical politically to:

- Form coalitions.
- Avoid petty disputes.
- Keep promises.
- Negotiate with those who hold different ideas and values.
- Be civil.
- Refuse to engage in character assassination.
- Communicate openly about positions and preferences
- Be willing to accommodate, compromise, and collaborate.
- Keep conflict functional.
- Allow people to save face.

- Tell the truth.
- Not promote zero-sum legitimacy.

Politics is power in action. Power is the ability to get somebody to do something they might not do ordinarily (Dahl, 1957). Like conflict and politics, power has both negative and positive faces (McClelland, 1970). Power may be *personalized* or *socialized,* meaning that people can be in it for themselves or have some sense that power is a necessary commodity in organizations and is necessary to do good things, not for oneself but for the organizational community and its aspirations. People have some measure of both types of power motives, but the question is whether personalized power motive can be appropriately inhibited at work. It needs to be. There is a considerable literature on power and OD and it all comes down to this: Promote socialized power motive and reduce personalized power motive.

There is one more issue with respect to power and OD. That is whether OD is the servant of higher authorities in organizations. Is OD a device to manipulate workers by giving them the illusion that they are empowered when they are caught up in the same old game of let's pretend what you say matters as long as it doesn't really threaten our control in this organization (compare with Berger and Luckmann, 1967; Nyhan, 2000)? It is fair to say some persons who call for change agents think they already know the problem in the organization, the thing to be fixed, or they think they just need help in what they truly believe is a better view of what is possible in the future— their outlook. They do not appreciate that these are tentative hypotheses. Sometimes subordinates perceive things differently and leaders have difficulty with what they think is a lack of support. They can blame the change agent or their staff or they can process the feedback and continue to support the change effort. Dealing with persons who bring in the change agent is delicate, political, and requires the ability to apply a measure of reflection in action, always renegotiating the relationship while supporting the leader's ability to process the new world emerging in the organization. It is an artful process. Change agents can do that or they can sell out to power. It is an ethical choice that OD practitioners make as individuals. There is nothing inherent in OD that automatically makes it a servant of power.

Moving Another Way

Organizational Development has come a long way and so have ideas about how to manage organizations. The evolution of management thinking involves a number of factors. From an OD point of view, there has been progress on more issues than others, but much has been accomplished (see Figure 7.1).

There are other issues that could be counterpoised in Figure 7.1. The important thing is that there be some recognition that things have not only changed, but taken together, the alterations have combined to evolve a fresh philosophy about structuring and leading organizations (Weisbord, 1987).

The new way of thinking about organizational management, first, demonstrates a shift away from command and control to more employee involvement. There is greater respect for what staff knows and the experience of employees is treated as valuable knowledge. Profiting from employee knowledge and creating forums where staff ideas are solicited is an ongoing activity in progressive institutions. The idea that superior know-how always exists at the top of organizational pyramids is discredited (Carnevale and Hummel, 1992). The fresh perspective, second, recognizes that organizations are systems embedded in and connected to other systems. That reality demands a different kind of leadership, a commitment to strategic thinking, and a concern about quality and customers. The word "customer" is maligned in public administration because of the fear that it means the field is embracing organizational models and processes inappropriate for the public enterprise. The worry is legitimate, but basic realities transfer. Public organizations are systems embedded in other systems and must pay attention, for instance, to politics of all kinds that shadow their operating domains. The public does have more standing as it presents itself before the government institution than the typical private-sector customer has when purchasing products from corporations. The taxpayer, strictly speaking, is not a customer. Still, the taxpayer is a client who rightfully expects courteous, caring, and quality service. Public organizations work without adequate resources and with insufficient public support. Indeed, government has become a hate object for some people, as events in Oklahoma City

FIGURE 7.1   Model of Change

Mechanistic organizations	Organic organizations
Power up the line	Power down the line
Specialized work	Teamwork
Reduced scope of action	Enlarged scope of action
Theory X assumptions	Theory Y assumptions
Telling	Participating
Quantity	Quality
Transactional Leadership	Transformational Leadership
Autocratic	Democratic
Performing according to the rules	Legitimizing learning from actual experience

demonstrated. Still, public organizations work to change in ways that make them responsive to all their stakeholders. They get better under difficult circumstances and examples of success exist everywhere (Terry, 1993; Cohen and Eimicke, 1998; Light, 1998).

The public sector is not immune to trends in the world of work. Most managers would not stand against teamwork. Many would support strategic planning and promote ethical politics. Like other people, managers would rather be followed because of what they stand for rather than the fear they can generate. Several managers would agree that their staffs know something and ought to be involved in what's going on. Although these things, and others that could be mentioned, seem obvious, it was not always this way. There has been a journey of change in thinking and operating in public organizations.

Summary and Conclusion

The most important thing that can be said about OD is that it has a point of view. Organizational Development has a strong commitment to making organizations more productive, but it will not accept instrumental gains as the only measure of organizational success. Human development matters in OD and work is seen as an activity that holds great promise for persons to actualize themselves. Organizations and their human resources are intimately related in the OD view and must collaborate for mutual gain. These ideals may seem beyond reach in reality, but consider the alternative. What is the consequence when organizations try to dominate staff, when people hate their jobs, when the climate is "us" versus "them"? There is no law of gravity about how organizations should be. The same applies to individuals. Attitude is chosen. The research is clear. Collaboration in social systems leads to better outcomes than confrontation. This is not a new idea, certainly. Chester Barnard (1938), in his classic work *The Functions of the Executive,* settled on one thought that is germane here. Organizations are social systems. Therefore, it is the primary function of the executive to get people to cooperate to achieve common goals. Much of what is considered management reform in recent years echoes this idea.

OD offers a number of methods to deal with an assortment of organizational problems. They can be applied in a pure fashion or worked as hybrids. Basically, they all affirm the worth of people. They involve employees in some way in identifying and solving problems. They are very process oriented, that is, how things are accomplished is an ongoing concern. They are optimistic that people can solve problems.

OD supports research and bases its activities on data. However, the type of research central to Organizational Development differs somewhat from what most behavioral scientists would consider proper investigation. OD is about Action Research; not research without action and not action without research. In other words, the data often comes from the client system and when employees come up with ideas on how to resolve difficulties, their notions are considered tentative hypotheses. The principal objective is not to retrieve data to publish in an academic journal. The information is intended to serve as a basis for action to solve real world problems. The research is the launching pad for doing something about a problem and seeing how it works. What actually happens in solving the problem is fed back into the client system where adjustments are made as necessary and action is taken based on client refinement of plans. These iterations repeat until the problem is solved. Action Research is the core technology of OD. Action Research incorporates OD's core values of humanism, optimism, and workplace democracy (French and Bell, 1999).

Third-party peacemaking is a long-standing intervention technique in OD. Conflict resolution has been addressed in this book, but it does not appear that dispute resolution techniques play a significant role in the curriculum at many schools of public administration. This is regrettable, given the fact that conflict is as pervasive in organizations as it is everywhere. Conflict resolution is a skill. Most people have learned their negotiation and mediation skills informally. Since OD is primarily concerned with change, dealing with disagreements, resistances, and defensive conduct are natural. An OD facilitator can help with these things, but organizations need to develop their own competencies in this area.

A word about trust is appropriate. OD requires high trust and intends to foster trust. Trust is another important issue in administration. How to build trust involves fairness in the management of incentive and reward systems, open communication, encouraging employee involvement, ethical conduct by leadership, allowing workers effective voice, and honoring commitments, that is, being credible (Carnevale, 1995). It is difficult to build trust in organizations but once it is lost it is doubly troublesome to get it back. Wise administrators know the importance of trust and pay attention to their relationships with subordinates, superiors, other organizational leaders, and important political actors.

There are a lot of questions about OD. How much change is enough or too much? Employees who have experienced reform after reform from management feel resentment about the idea of change initiatives because of the constant new methods that have been overly idealized by organizational authorities. Expectations have been overstated and results are often poor. Another question is, what is the sticking power of change initiatives? To what extent do they become embedded in the culture? More follow-up research on case studies reported in the public administration literature that are invariably positive about

OD-like interventions might become more longitudinal. As indicated previously, what is the experience of OD in organizations with a high degree of unionization? Is there a need for the development of interventions that specifically target the problem of organizational learning? To what extent can recent management reforms like TQM, reinvention, and reengineering be considered OD?

OD is a philosophy. That is the conclusion. It has, whether it recognizes it or not, strong existential connections. It values the self. It sees organizations and staff always in the process of becoming. OD's affection for all things democratic supports the ideas of freedom and choice. OD believes that people have a right to personal development and that work is an important activity in that development. An old saying states that work mediates between man and God. Finally, OD is uplifting, high trust, and optimistic about the nature of people. It brings these values to the workplace. As stated earlier, OD has a point of view. OD has a vision for a better future for people. Public administrators are well served by learning about the field and putting its ideas into practice.

References

Chapter 1

Argyris, Chris. *Personality and Organizational: The Conflict Between System and the Individual.* New York: Harper, 1957.

Barnard, Chester Irving. *The Functions of the Executive.* Cambridge, Mass.: Harvard University Press, 1938.

Bass, Bernard M. *Leadership and Performance Beyond Expectations.* New York and London: Free Press; Collier Macmillan, 1985.

Bennis, Warren G. *Organization Development: Its Nature, Origins, and Prospects.* Addison-Wesley Series on Organization Development. Reading, Mass.: Addison-Wesley, 1969.

Bertalanffy, Ludwig von. "The Theory of Open Systems in Physics and Biology." *Science* 3 (1950): 23–28.

_____. "General Systems Theory." *General Systems* 1 (1956): 1–10.

Braverman, Harry. *Labor and Monopoly Capital: The Degradation of Work in the Twentieth Century.* New York: Monthly Review Press, 1974.

Bruce, Raymon, and Sherman M. Wyman. *Changing Organizations: Practicing Action Training and Research.* Thousand Oaks, Calif.: Sage Publications, 1998.

Burke, W. Warner. *Organization Development: A Normative View.* Addison-Wesley Series on Organization Development. Reading, Mass.: Addison-Wesley, 1982.

Burrell, Gibson, and Gareth Morgan. *Sociological Paradigms and Organisational Analysis: Elements of the Sociology of Corporate Life.* Suffolk: Ipswich Book Company, 1979.

Carnevale, Anthony Patrick. *America and the New Economy: How New Competitive Standards Are Radically Changing American Workplaces.* 1st ed., Jossey-Bass Management Series. San Francisco: Jossey-Bass, 1990.

Conger, Jay Alden. *The Charismatic Leader: Behind the Mystique of Exceptional Leadership.* 1st ed., Jossey-Bass Management Series. San Francisco: Jossey-Bass, 1989.

Deal, Terrence E., and Allan A. Kennedy. *Corporate Cultures: The Rites and Rituals of Corporate Life.* Reading, Mass.: Addison-Wesley, 1982.

Deming, W. Edwards. *Out of the Crisis.* Cambridge, Mass.: MIT Center for Advanced Engineering Study, 1986.

French, Wendell. "Organizational Development Objectives, Assumptions, and Strategies." *California Management Review* 12 (1969): 23–34.

French, Wendell L., and Cecil Bell. *Organization Development: Behavioral Science Interventions for Organization Improvement.* 6th ed. Upper Saddle River, N.J.: Prentice-Hall, 1999.

Golembiewski, Robert T. *Humanizing Public Organizations: Perspectives on Doing Better-Than-Average When Average Ain't at All Bad.* Mt. Airy, Md.: Lomond, 1985.

Gore, A. "From Red Tape to Results: Creating a Government That Works Better and Costs Less." Washington, D.C.: National Performance Review, 1993.

Guillén, Mauro F. *Models of Management: Work, Authority, and a Comparative Perspective.* Chicago: University of Chicago Press, 1994.

Hackman, J. Richard, and Greg R. Oldham. *Work Redesign, Organization Development.* Reading, Mass.: Addison-Wesley, 1980.

Herzberg, Frederick. *Work and the Nature of Man.* Cleveland, Ohio: World Publishing Company, 1966.

Juran, J. M. *Juran on Planning for Quality.* New York and London: Free Press; Collier Macmillan, 1988.

Kilmann, Ralph H. *Beyond the Quick Fix: Managing Five Tracks to Organizational Success.* 1st ed., a joint publication in the Jossey-Bass Management Series and the Jossey-Bass Social and Behavioral Science Series. San Francisco: Jossey-Bass, 1984.

Kilmann, Ralph H., Mary J. Saxton, Roy Serpa, and University of Pittsburgh Program in Corporate Culture. *Gaining Control of the Corporate Culture.* 1st ed., a joint publication in the Jossey-Bass Management Series and the Jossey-Bass Social and Behavioral Science Series. San Francisco: Jossey-Bass, 1985.

Lewin, Kurt. "Frontiers in Group Dynamics: Concept, Method, and Reality in Social Science; Social Equilibria and Social Change." *Human Relations* 1, no. 1 (1947): 5–41.

Likert, Rensis. *New Patterns of Management.* New York: McGraw-Hill, 1961.

Maslow, Abraham H. *Eupsychian Management: A Journal.* The Irwin-Dorsey Series in Behavioral Science. Homewood, Ill.: R. D. Irwin, 1965.

McGill, Michael E. "The Evolution of Organization Development: 1947–1960." *Public Administration Review* 34 (1974): 58–105.

McGregor, Douglas. *The Human Side of Enterprise.* New York: McGraw-Hill, 1960.

Osborne, David, and Ted Gaebler. *Reinventing Government: How the Entrepreneurial Spirit Is Transforming the Public Sector.* Reading, Mass.: Addison-Wesley, 1992.

Ouchi, William G. *Theory Z: How American Business Can Meet the Japanese Challenge.* Reading, Mass.: Addison-Wesley, 1981.

Peters, Thomas J., and Robert H. Waterman. *In Search of Excellence: Lessons from America's Best-Run Companies.* 1st ed. New York: Harper and Row, 1982.

Quinn, Robert E. *Deep Change: Discovering the Leader Within.* 1st ed., Jossey-Bass Business and Management Series. San Francisco: Jossey-Bass, 1996.

Schachter, Hindy Lauer. *Frederick Taylor and the Public Administration Community: A Reevaluation.* Suny Series in Public Administration. Albany: State University of New York Press, 1989.

Senge, Peter M. *The Fifth Discipline: The Art and Practice of the Learning Organization.* 1st ed. New York: Doubleday, 1990.

Tannenbaum, Robert, Sheldon Davis, and University of California Los Angeles Institute of Industrial Relations. *Values, Man, and Organizations.* Reprint. Institute of Industrial Relations 202. Los Angeles: Institute of Industrial Relations, University of California, 1969.

Taylor, Frederick Winslow. *The Principles of Scientific Management.* New York and London: Harper and Brothers, 1911.

Thayer, Frederick. "Organizational Theory As Epistemology: Transcending Hierarchy." In *Organization Theory and the New Public Administration,* edited by Carl Bellone, 113–139. Boston: Allyn and Bacon, 1980.

Trist, E. L., and K. W. Bamforth. "Some Social and Psychological Consequences of the Longwall Method of Coal-Getting." *Human Relations* 4, no. 1 (1951): 3–38.

Weber, Max, Hans Heinrich Gerth, and C. Wright Mills. From *Max Weber: Essays in Sociology.* New York: Oxford University Press, 1946.

Weisbord, Marvin Ross. *Productive Workplaces: Organizing and Managing for Dignity, Meaning, and Community.* 1st ed., Jossey-Bass Management Series. San Francisco: Jossey-Bass, 1987.

Wilson, Woodrow. "Study of Administration." *Political Science Quarterly* 2 (June 1887): 197–222.

Chapter 2

Argyris, Chris. *Personality and Organization: The Conflict Between System and the Individual.* New York: Harper, 1957.

_____. "Some Limits of Rational Man Organizational Theory." *Public Administration Review* 33, no. 3 (1973): 253–266.

_____. "Organizational Man: Rational and Self-Actualizing." *Public Administration Review* 33, no. 4 (1973): 354–357.

Bennis, Warren G. *Organization Development: Its Nature, Origins, and Prospects,* Addison-Wesley Series on Organization Development. Reading, Mass.: Addison-Wesley, 1969.

Bozeman, Barry. *All Organizations Are Public: Bridging Public and Private Organizational Theories.* 1st ed., Jossey-Bass Management Series. San Francisco: Jossey-Bass, 1987.

Bruce, Raymon R., and Sherman M. Wyman. *Changing Organizations: Practicing Action Training and Research.* Thousand Oaks, Calif.: Sage Publications, 1998.

Carnevale, David G. *Trustworthy Government: Leadership and Management Strategies for Building Trust and High Performance.* 1st ed., Jossey-Bass Public Administration Series. San Francisco: Jossey-Bass, 1995.

Golembiewski, Robert T. *Men, Management, and Morality: Toward a New Organizational Ethic.* McGraw-Hill Series in Management. New York: McGraw-Hill, 1965.

_____. "Organization Development in Public Agencies: Perspectives on Theory and Practice." *Public Administration Review* 29 (1969): 367–368.

_____. *Renewing Organizations: The Laboratory Approach to Planned Change.* Itasca, Ill.: F. E. Peacock, 1972.

_____. *Approaches to Planned Change, Public Administration and Public Policy.* New York: M. Dekker, 1979.

_____. *Humanizing Public Organizations: Perspectives on Doing Better-Than-Average When Average Ain't at All Bad.* Mt. Airy, Md.: Lomond, 1985.

_____. *Practical Public Management, Public Administration and Public Policy.* New York: M. Dekker, 1995.

Golembiewski, Robert T., Carl W. Proehl, and David Sinck. "Estimating Success of OD Applications." *Training and Development Journal* 72, no. 2 (1982): 86–95.

Golembiewski, Robert T., and Ben-Chu Sun. "Positive Findings Bias in Qwl Studies." *Journal of Management* 16 (1990): 665–674.

Harmon, M. M. and Mayer, R. T. *Organization Theory and Public Administration.* New York: Little, Brown, and Company, 1986.

Herzberg, Frederick. *Work and the Nature of Man.* Cleveland, Ohio: World Publishing Company, 1966.

Hummel, Ralph. *The Bureaucratic Experience.* New York: St. Martin's Press, 1987.

Likert, Rensis. *New Patterns of Management.* New York: McGraw-Hill, 1961.

Maslow, Abraham H. *Motivation and Personality.* 1st ed., Harper's Psychological Series. New York: Harper, 1954.

_____. *Toward a Psychology of Being.* Insight Book 5. Princeton, N.J.: Van Nostrand, 1962.

_____. *Eupsychian Management: A Journal.* The Irwin-Dorsey Series in Behavioral Science. Homewood, Ill.: R. D. Irwin, 1965.

McGregor, Douglas. *The Human Side of Enterprise.* New York: McGraw-Hill, 1960.

Rainey, Hal G. *Understanding and Managing Public Organizations.* 2nd ed., The Jossey-Bass Public Nonprofit and Public Management Series. San Francisco: Jossey-Bass, 1997.

Robertson, P. J., and S. J. Seneviratne. "Outcomes of Planned Organizational Change in the Public Sector: A Meta-Analytic Comparison to the Private Sector." *Public Administration Review* 55 (1995): 547–558.

Schwartz, Howard S. *Narcissistic Process and Corporate Decay: The Theory of the Organization Ideal.* New York: New York University Press, 1990.

Simon, Herbert A. "Organizational Man: Rational or Self-Actualizing?" *Public Administration Review* 33, no. 4 (1973): 346–353.

Chapter 3

Argyris, Chris. *Personality and Organization: The Conflict Between System and the Individual.* New York: Harper, 1957.

Barker, Joel Arthur. *Paradigms: The Business of Discovering the Future.* 1st ed. New York: HarperBusiness, 1992.

Bass, Bernard M. *Leadership and Performance Beyond Expectations.* New York and London: Free Press; Collier Macmillan, 1985.

Bennis, Warren G., and Burt Nanus. *Leaders: The Strategies for Taking Charge.* 1st ed. New York: Harper and Row, 1985.

Bion, Wilfred R. *Experiences in Groups, and Other Papers.* London: Tavistock, 1961.

Bolman, Lee G., and Terrence E. Deal. *Reframing Organizations: Artistry, Choice, and Leadership.* 1st ed., Jossey-Bass Management Series. San Francisco: Jossey-Bass, 1991.

Bryson, John M., and Sharon R. Anderson. "Applying Large-Group Interaction Methods in the Planning and Implementation of Major Change Efforts." *Public Administration Review* 60, no. 2 (2000): 143–163.

Burns, J. M. *Leadership.* New York: Harper and Row, 1978.

Campbell, Joseph. *The Hero with a Thousand Faces.* Princeton, N.J.: Princeton University Press, 1973.

Carnavale, David G. "A Model of Organizational Trust: A Case Study in Florida State Government." Ph.D. diss., Florida State University, 1988.

_____. *Trustworthy Government: Leadership and Management Strategies for Building Trust and High Performance.* 1st ed., Jossey-Bass Public Administration Series. San Francisco: Jossey-Bass, 1995.

Conger, J. A., and R. N. Kanungo. "Toward a Behavioral Theory of Charasmatic Leadership in Organizational Settings." *Academy of Management Review* 12 (1987): 637–647.

Festinger, Leon. *A Theory of Cognitive Dissonance.* Stanford, Calif.: Stanford University Press, 1957.

French, Wendell L., and Cecil Bell. *Organization Development: Behavioral Science Interventions for Organization Improvement.* 6th ed. Upper Saddle River, N.J.: Prentice-Hall, 1999.

Freud, Sigmund. "Beyond the Pleasure Principle." In *The Standard Edition of the Complete Psychological Works of Sigmund Freud,* edited by J. Strachey. London: Hogarth, 1920.

Gibson, James L., John M. Ivancevich, and James H. Donnelly. *Organizations: Behavior, Structure, Processes.* Boston, Mass.: Irwin, McGraw-Hill, 2000.

Heatherton, T. F., and P. A. Nichols. "Personal Accounts of Successful Versus Failed Attempts at Life Change." *Personality and Social Psychology Bulletin* 29, no. 6 (1994): 664–675.

Janis, Irving Lester. *Victims of Groupthink: A Psychological Study of Foreign-Policy Decisions and Fiascoes.* Boston: Houghton Mifflin, 1972.

Judson, Arnold S. *Changing Behavior in Organizations: Minimizing Resistance to Change.* Cambridge, Mass.: Basil Blackwell, 1991.

Kets de Vries, Manford F. R., and Katharina Balazs Insead. "Transforming the Mind-Set of the Organization: A Clinical Perspsective." *Administration Society* 30, no. 6 (1999): 640–675.

Lewin, Kurt. "Frontiers in Group Dynamics, Part 2: Channels of Group Life: Social Planning and Action Research." *Human Relations* 1 (1947): 143–153.

Micklethwait, John, and Adrian Wooldridge. *The Witch Doctors: Making Sense of the Management Gurus.* London: Heinemann, 1996.

Morgan, Gareth. *Images of Organization.* 2nd ed. Thousand Oaks, Calif.: Sage Publications, 1997.

Quinn, Robert E. *Deep Change: Discovering the Leader Within.* 1st ed., Jossey-Bass Business and Management Series. San Francisco: Jossey-Bass, 1996.

Quinn, Robert E., and Kim S. Cameron. *Paradox and Transformation: Toward a Theory of Change in Organization and Management.* Ballinger Series on Innovation and Organization Change. Cambridge, Mass.: Ballinger, 1988.

Rainey, Hal G. "Using Comparisons of Public and Private Organizations to Access Innovative Attitudes Among Members of Organizations." *Public Productivity and Management Review* 23, no. 2 (1999): 130–158.

Rogers, Carl R. *Client-Centered Therapy, Its Current Practice, Implications, and Theory.* The Houghton Mifflin Psychological Series. Boston: Houghton Mifflin, 1951.

_____. *Freedom to Learn: A View of What Education Might Become, Studies of the Person.* Columbus, Ohio: C. E. Merrill, 1969.

Schein, Edgar H. *Process Consultation.* Vol. 2, *Lessons for Managers and Consultants.* Addison-Wesley Series on Organization Development. Reading, Mass.,: Addison-Wesley, 1987.

_____. *Process Consultation.* Vol. I, *Its Role in Organization Development.* 2nd ed., Addison-Wesley Series on Organization Development. Reading, Mass.: Addison-Wesley, 1988.

Senge, Peter M., Richard Ross, Bryan Smith, Charlotte Roberts, and Art Kleiner. *The Fifth Discipline Fieldbook.* New York: Doubleday, 1994.

Shapiro, Eileen C. *Fad Surfing in the Boardroom: Reclaiming the Courage to Manage in the Age of Instant Answers.* Reading, Mass.: Addison-Wesley, 1995.

Weisbord, Marvin Ross. *Productive Workplaces: Organizing and Managing for Dignity, Meaning, and Community.* 1st ed., Jossey-Bass Management Series. San Francisco: Jossey-Bass, 1987.

Chapter 4

Appelbaum, Eileen, and Rosemary L. Batt. *The New American Workplace: Transforming Work Systems in the United States.* Ithaca, N.Y.: ILR Press, 1994.

Argyris, Chris. *Reasoning, Learning, and Action: Individual and Organizational.* 1st ed., a joint publication in the Jossey-Bass Series in Social and Behavioral Science and in Management, Training, and Development. San Francisco: Jossey-Bass, 1982.

_____. *Knowledge for Action: A Guide to Overcoming Barriers to Organizational Change.* 1st ed., a joint publication in the Jossey-Bass Management Series and the Jossey-Bass Social and Behavioral Science Series. San Francisco: Jossey-Bass, 1993.

Argyris, Chris, Robert Putnam, and Diana McLain Smith. *Action Science.* 1st ed., Jossey-Bass Social and Behavioral Science Series. San Francisco: Jossey-Bass, 1985.

Bacon, Francis. *A Selection of His Works.* Indianapolis, Ind.: Bobbs-Merrill Educational Publishing, 1965.

Berger, Peter L., and Thomas Luckmann. *The Social Construction of Reality: A Treatise in the Sociology of Knowledge.* Garden City, N.Y.: Anchor Books, 1966.

Braverman, Harry. *Labor and Monopoly Capital: The Degradation of Work in the Twentieth Century.* New York: Monthly Review Press, 1974.

Bruce, Raymon, and Sherman M. Wyman. *Changing Organizations: Practicing Action Training and Research.* Thousand Oaks, Calif.: Sage Publications, 1998.

Carnevale, Anthony Patrick. *America and the New Economy: How New Competitive Standards Are Radically Changing American Workplaces.* 1st ed., Jossey-Bass Management Series. San Francisco: Jossey-Bass, 1991.

Carnevale, David G. *Trustworthy Government: Leadership and Management Strategies for Building Trust and High Performance.* 1st ed., Jossey-Bass Public Administration Series. San Francisco: Jossey-Bass, 1995.

———. "A Symposium: The Human Capital Challenge in Government." *Review of Public Personnel Administration* 16, no. 3 (1996): 5–13.

French, Wendell L., and Cecil Bell. *Organization Development: Behavioral Science Interventions for Organization Improvement.* 6th ed. Upper Saddle River, N.J.: Prentice-Hall, 1999.

McGregor, Douglas. *The Human Side of Enterprise.* New York: McGraw-Hill, 1960.

Robson, Colin. *Real World Research: A Resource for Social Scientists and Practitioner-Researchers.* Oxford, UK; Cambridge, Mass.: Blackwell, 1993.

Salamon, Lester M. "Why Human Capital? Why Now?" In *Human Capital and America's Future: An Economic Strategy for the '90s,* edited by David W. Hornbeck and Lester M. Salamon, 1–39. Baltimore: Johns Hopkins University Press, 1991.

Senge, Peter M. *The Fifth Discipline: The Art and Practice of the Learning Organization.* 1st ed. New York: Doubleday, 1990.

Taylor, Frederick Winslow. *The Principles of Scientific Management.* New York and London: Harper and Brothers, 1911.

Watkins, Karen E., and Victoria J. Marsick. *Sculpting the Learning Organization: Lessons in the Art and Science of Systemic Change.* 1st ed., Jossey-Bass Management Series. San Francisco: Jossey-Bass, 1993.

Chapter 5

Argyris, Chris. *Knowledge for Action: A Guide to Overcoming Barriers to Organizational Change.* 1st ed., a joint publication in the Jossey-Bass Management Series and the Jossey-Bass Social and Behavioral Science Series. San Francisco: Jossey-Bass, 1993.

Barnard, Chester Irving. *The Functions of the Executive.* Cambridge, Mass.: Harvard University Press, 1938.

Bendix, Reinhard. *Work and Authority in Industry: Ideologies of Management in the Course of Industrialization.* New York: Harper and Row, 1963.

Bion, Wilfred R. *Experiences in Groups, and Other Papers.* London: Tavistock, 1961.

Bryson, John M., and Sharon R. Anderson. "Applying Large-Group Interaction Methods in the Planning and Implementation of Major Change Efforts." *Public Administration Review* 60, no. 2 (2000): 143–163.

Carnevale, David G. *Trustworthy Government: Leadership and Management Strategies for Building Trust and High Performance.* 1st ed., Jossey-Bass Public Administration Series. San Francisco: Jossey-Bass, 1995.

Deming, W. Edwards. *Out of the Crisis.* Cambridge, Mass.: MIT Center for Advanced Engineering Study, 1986.

Fayol, Henri. *General and Industrial Management.* New York: Pitman, 1949.

Gore, A. "From Red Tape to Results: Creating a Government That Works Better and Costs Less." Washington, D.C.: National Performance Review, 1993.

Hammer, Michael, and James Champy. *Reengineering the Corporation: A Manifesto for Business Revolution.* 1st ed. New York: HarperBusiness, 1993.

Harvey, Jerry B. *The Abilene Paradox and Other Meditations on Management.* Lexington, Mass., and San Diego: Lexington Books; University Associates, 1988.

Homans, George Caspar. *The Human Group.* New York: Harcourt Brace, 1950.

Janis, Irving Lester. *Groupthink: Psychological Studies of Policy Decisions and Fiascoes.* 2nd ed. Boston: Houghton Mifflin, 1982.

Juran, J. M. *Juran on Planning for Quality.* New York and London: Free Press; Collier Macmillan, 1988.

Katzenbach, Jon R., and Douglas K. Smith. *The Wisdom of Teams: Creating the High-Performance Organization.* Boston: Harvard Business School Press, 1993.

Mayo, Elton, and Harvard University Graduate School of Business Administration, Division of Research. *The Human Problems of an Industrial Civilization.* Boston: Division of Research Graduate School of Business Administration, Harvard University, 1946.

Micklethwait, John, and Adrian Wooldridge. *The Witch Doctors: Making Sense of the Management Gurus.* London: Heinemann, 1996.

Mohrman, Susan Albers, Susan G. Cohen, Allan M. Mohrman Jr., and University of Southern California Center for Effective Organizations. *Designing Team-Based Organizations: New Forms for Knowledge Work.* 1st ed., the Jossey-Bass Management Series. San Francisco: Jossey-Bass, 1995.

Organ, E. "A Communitarian Approach to Local Governance." *National Civic Review* (summer 1993): 226–233.

Osborne, David, and Ted Gaebler. *Reinventing Government: How the Entrepreneurial Spirit Is Transforming the Public Sector.* Reading, Mass.: Addison-Wesley, 1992.

Ouchi, William G. *Theory Z: How American Business Can Meet the Japanese Challenge.* Reading, Mass.: Addison-Wesley, 1981.

Parker, L. D. "Control in Organizational Life: The Contribution of Mary Parker Follett." *Academy of Management Review* 9, no. 4 (1984): 136–145.

Peters, Thomas J., and Robert H. Waterman. *In Search of Excellence: Lessons from America's Best-Run Companies.* 1st ed. New York: Harper and Row, 1982.

Quigley, Barbara. "Residents Seek Answers to Roadway Danger." *Norman Transcript,* September 28, 2000, 1–2.

Riccucci, Norma. "The 'Old' Public Management Versus the 'New' Public Management: Where Does Public Administration Fit In?" *Public Administration Review* 61, no. 2 (2001): 172–176.

Roethlisberger, Fritz Jules, William John Dickson, and Harold A. Wright. *Management and the Worker: An Account of a Research Program Conducted by the Western Electric Company, Hawthorne Works, Chicago.* Cambridge, Mass.: Harvard University Press, 1939.

Schachter, Stanley, Norris Ellertson, Dorothy McBride, and Doris Gregory. "An Experimental Study of Cohesiveness and Productivity." *Human Relations* (1951): 229–239.

Senge, Peter M. *The Fifth Discipline: The Art and Practice of the Learning Organization.* 1st ed. New York: Doubleday, 1990.

Sundstrom, Eric D., and associates. *Supporting Work Team Effectiveness: Best Management Practices for Fostering High Performance.* 1st ed., the Jossey-Bass Business and Management Series. San Francisco: Jossey-Bass, 1999.

Sundstrom, Eric D., K. Demeuse, and D. Furrell. "Work Teams: Applications and Effectiveness." *American Psychologist* 45, no. 2 (1990): 120–133.

Taylor, Frederick Winslow. *The Principles of Scientific Management.* New York and London: Harper and Brothers, 1911.

_____. *Shop Management.* New York: Harper, 1919.

Vigoda, Eran, and Robert T. Golembiewski. "Citizenship Behavior and the Spirit of New Managerialsm: A Theoretical Framework and Challenge for Governance." *American Review of Public Administration* 31, no. 3 (2001): 273–296.

Weber, Max, Hans Heinrich Gerth, and C. Wright Mills. From *Max Weber: Essays in Sociology.* New York: Oxford University Press, 1946.

Yeatts, Dale E., and Cloyd Hyten. *High-Performing Self-Managed Work Teams: A Comparison of Theory to Practice.* Thousand Oaks, Calif.: Sage Publications, 1998.

Chapter 6

Allcorn, Seth. *Anger in the Workplace: Understanding the Causes of Aggression and Violence.* Westport, Conn.: Quorum Books, 1994.

Argyris, Chris. *Knowledge for Action: A Guide to Overcoming Barriers to Organizational Change.* 1st ed., a joint publication in the Jossey-Bass Management Series and the Jossey-Bass Social and Behavioral Science Series. San Francisco: Jossey-Bass, 1993.

Bandura, Albert. *Self-Efficacy in Changing Societies.* Cambridge and New York: Cambridge University Press, 1995.

Blake, Robert Rogers, and Jane Srygley Mouton. *The Managerial Grid: Key Orientations for Achieving Production Through People.* Houston: Gulf, 1964.

Bohm, D., Factor, D., and P. Garret. *Dialogue: A Proposal.* http://world.std.com /_lo/bohm/0000.html, 1991.

Bohm, David, and Lee Nichol. *On Dialogue.* London and New York: Routledge, 1996.

Buber, Martin. *I and Thou.* 2d ed. New York: Scribner, 1958.

Geen, Russell G., and Edward I. Donnerstein. *Human Aggression: Theories, Research, and Implications for Social Policy.* San Diego: Academic Press, 1998.

Harvey, Jerry B. *The Abilene Paradox and Other Meditations on Management.* Lexington, Mass., and San Diego: Lexington Books; University Associates, 1988.

Luke, Jeffrey Scott. *Catalytic Leadership: Strategies for an Interconnected World.* 1st ed., Jossey-Bass Nonprofit and Public Management Series. San Francisco: Jossey-Bass, 1998.

National Mediation Board. "Interest-Based Bargaining: A Structured Problem-Solving Approach." Washington, D.C.: National Mediation Board, 1994.

Pruitt, Dean G., and Peter J. Carnevale. *Negotiation in Social Conflict, Mapping Social Psychology Series.* Pacific Grove, Calif.: Brooks/Cole, 1993.

Rahim, M. A. "A Measure of Styles of Handling Interpersonal Conflict." *Journal of Social Psychology* (1983).

Rotter, Julian B., and Dorothy J. Hochreich. *Personality.* Scott Foresman Basic Psychological Concepts Series. Glenview, Ill.: Scott Foresman, 1975.

Rubin, Jeffrey Z., Dean G. Pruitt, and Sung Hee Kim. *Social Conflict: Escalation, Stalemate, and Settlement.* 2nd ed., McGraw-Hill Series in Social Psychology. New York: McGraw-Hill, 1994.

Ruble, T. L., and K. W. Thomas. "Support for a Two-Dimensional Model of Conflict Behavior." *Organizational Behavior and Human Performance* 16 (1976): 143–155.

Thomas, K. W., and R. H. Kilmann. *Thomas-Kilmann Conflict Mode Instrument.* Tuxedo, N.Y.: Vicom, 1974.

Zuker, Elaina. *Mastering Assertiveness Skills: Power and Positive Influence at Work.* New York: American Management Association, 1983.

Chapter 7

Appelbaum, Eileen, and Rosemary L. Batt. *The New American Workplace: Transforming Work Systems in the United States.* Ithaca, N.Y.: ILR Press, 1994.

Argyris, Chris. *Understanding Organizational Behavior.* Homewood, Ill.: Dorsey Press, 1960.

Barnard, Chester Irving. *The Functions of the Executive.* Cambridge, Mass.: Harvard University Press, 1938.

Bass, Bernard M. *Leadership and Performance Beyond Expectations.* New York and London: Free Press; Collier Macmillan, 1985.

Berger, Peter L., and Thomas Luckmann. *The Social Construction of Reality: A Treatise in the Sociology of Knowledge.* Garden City, N.Y.: Anchor Books, 1967.

Carnevale, David G. *Trustworthy Government: Leadership and Management Strategies for Building Trust and High Performance.* 1st ed., Jossey-Bass Public Administration Series. San Francisco: Jossey-Bass, 1995.

Carnevale, D., and R. Hummel. "In the Age of the Smart Machine: The Future of Work and Power." *Public Administration Review* (1992): 213–214.

Cohen, Steven, and William B. Eimicke. *Tools for Innovators: Creative Strategies for Managing Public Sector Organizations.* 1st ed., Jossey-Bass Nonprofit and Public Management Series. San Francisco: Jossey-Bass, 1998.

Creed, W. E. Douglas, and E. Raymond Miles. "A Conceptual Framework Linking Organizational Forms, Managerial Philosophies, and the Opportunity Costs of Controls." In *Trust in Organizations: Frontiers of Theory and Research,* edited by Roderick Moreland Kramer and Tom R. Tyler. Thousand Oaks, Calif.: Sage Publications, 1996.

Dahl, R. A. "The Concept of Power." *Behavioral Science* (1957): 202–203.

Deutsch, Morton. *The Resolution of Conflict: Constructive and Destructive Processes.* New Haven, Conn.: Yale University Press, 1973.

Fox, Alan. *Beyond Contract; Work, Power and Trust Relations, Society Today and Tomorrow.* London: Faber and Faber, 1974.

French, Wendell L., and Cecil Bell. *Organization Development: Behavioral Science Interventions for Organization Improvement.* 6th ed. Upper Saddle River, N.J.: Prentice-Hall, 1999.

Golembiewski, Robert T. "Od Perspectives on High Performance: Some Good News and Some Bad News About Merit Pay." *Review of Public Personnel Administration* 7 (1986): 9–27.

Golembiewski, Robert T., and Mark L. McConkie. "The Centrality of Interpersonal Trust in Group Processes." In *Theories of Group Processes: Wiley Series on Individuals, Groups, and Organizations,* edited by Cary L. Cooper. London and New York: Wiley, 1975.

Kearney, Richard C., and David G. Carnevale. *Labor Relations in the Public Sector.* 3rd ed. New York: Marcel Dekker, 2001.

Light, Paul Charles. *Sustaining Innovation: Creating Nonprofit and Government Organizations That Innovate Naturally.* 1st ed., Jossey-Bass Nonprofit and Public Management Series. San Francisco: Jossey-Bass, 1998.

Likert, Rensis. *The Human Organization: Its Management and Value.* New York: McGraw-Hill, 1967.

Marsden, David. "Understanding the Role of Interfirm Institutions in Sustaining Trust Within Employment Relationship." In *Trust Within and Between Organizations: Conceptual Issues and Empirical Applications,* edited by Christel Lane and Reinhard Bachmann, 173–203. Oxford and New York: Oxford University Press, 2000.

Maslow, Abraham H. *Motivation and Personality.* 1st ed., Harper's Psychological Series. New York: Harper, 1954.

McClelland. "The Two Faces of Power." *Journal of International Affairs* 24, no. 1 (1970): 26–47.

McGregor, Douglas. *The Human Side of Enterprise.* New York: McGraw-Hill, 1960.

Mellinger, G. D. "Interpersonal Trust Is a Factor in Communication." *Journal of Abnormal Social Psychology* 52 (1956): 304–309.

Menzel, Donald C. "Ethics Versus Evil: Is It Before or After Midnight in the Garden of Ethics and Evil?" *American Review of Public Administration* 31, no. 3 (2001): 340–350.

Nyhan, Ronald C. "Changing the Paradigm: Trust and Its Role in Public Sector Organizations." *American Review of Public Administration* 30, no. 1 (2000): 87–109.

Reich, Robert B. *Tales of a New America.* 1st ed. New York: Times Books, 1987.

Terry, Robert W. *Authentic Leadership: Courage in Action.* 1st ed., a joint publication in the Jossey-Bass Public Administration Series, the Jossey-Bass Nonprofit Sector Series, and the Jossey Bass Management Series. San Francisco: Jossey-Bass, 1993.

Weber, Max, Alexander Morell Henderson, and Talcott Parsons. *The Theory of Social and Economic Organization.* Glencoe, Ill.: Free Press, 1947.

Weisbord, Marvin Ross. *Productive Workplaces: Organizing and Managing for Dignity, Meaning, and Community.* 1st ed., Jossey-Bass Management Series. San Francisco: Jossey-Bass, 1987.

Yukl, Gary A. *Leadership in Organizations.* 3rd ed. Englewood Cliffs, N.J.: Prentice-Hall, 1994.

Zand, D. E. "Trust and Managerial Problem Solving." *Administrative Science Quarterly* 17 (1972): 229–239.

ABOUT THE AUTHOR

David G. Carnevale is a professor of human relations and political science at the University of Oklahoma. He also served as the University's Samuel Roberts Noble Presidential Professor. He received his B.A. degree in political science from the University of Maine–Portland in 1969 and his Ph.D. in public administration in 1989 from Florida State University.

Professor Carnevale is the author of *Trustworthy Government* and coauthor with Richard Kearney on Kearney's third edition of *Labor Relations in the Public Sector*. Professor Carnevale has published extensively in refereed journals and has contributed chapters to several books. He is published, for instance, in *Public Administrative Review, American Review of Public Administration, Review of Public Personnel Administration, International Journal of Public Administration,* and *Public Productivity and Management Review.* Dr. Carnevale has served on the board of editors of *JPART* and is currently on the editorial board of *Public Administrative Review* and *Review of Public Personnel Administration.*

Dr. Carnevale teaches Organizational Development, conflict resolution, mediation, and organizational behavior at the University of Oklahoma. His primary research interest is in the area of Alternative Dispute Resolution (ADR).

Dr. Carnevale has served as the executive director of the Maine State Employees Association, operations administrator of the California State Employees Associations, and international union area director for the American Federation of State, County, and Municipal Employees (AFSCME) of the AFL-CIO. He has considerable negotiations experience and is a practicing mediator and organizational consultant.

INDEX

Taylor, Frederick, continued
  and customers, 87–88
  and mental revolution, 6
  and scientific management, 65–66
Team building, 63
Teams, 15–16, 80–83
  definition of, 79–80
  and tools for change, 23(table)
  See also Groups
Teamwork, 71, 73
T-Groups, 10–11. *See also* Groups
Thinking, 67
  one-sided, 100
  open systems, 12
  See also Management thinking
Third-party peacemaking, 26–30,
  102, 103–104, 124
Three-step process, and change, 9–10
Time-and-motion studies, 5
TL. *See* Transformational Leadership
Total organization
  and tools for change, 23(table)
Total Quality Management (TQM),
  15, 63, 84. *See also* Business
  management; Management
  reform; Management thinking;
  Public management; Scientific
  management
Touchy-feely label, 13, 113
TQM. *See* Total Quality Management
Training, 68–69
Transformational Leadership (TL),
  117–118
Trust, 30, 56–58, 72, 73, 90, 124
  in government, 97(n1)
  problem of, 114–116

Truth, 102, 118
Twelve-step program, 51

Unfreezing stage, 9, 46
Unresolved prior conflict, 28,
  100–101

Vigoda, Eran, 85–86
Visioning exercises, 63

Waterman, Robert, 83
Ways of knowing, 14
Weber, Max, 81
  and ideal-type bureaucracy,
  5–6
Weisbord, Marvin
  and change, process of, 44–47,
  45(figure)
  and "four-room apartment,"
  44–47, 45(figure)
Western Electric Company,
  82
Win-win techniques, 27
Wisdom
  and experience, 2
Work, meaning of, 6, 7
Work culture
  authoritarian vs. participatory,
  66–67
Work groups
  virtues of, 90–93
  See also Groups
Work teams, 15–16
  self-directed, 80–83
  See also Teams
Wyman, Sherman, 35